CONTENTS

Acknowledgments 2
Abbreviations 2

Chapter 1: Background to a Bloody War 3
Chapter 2: Two Armies 7
Chapter 3: From Border War to Invasion 17
Chapter 4: The Invasion of Khuzestan 23
Chapter 5: The Iranians Strike Back 44
Chapter 6: The Writing on the Wall 55
Chapter 7: Disaster for Iraq 62

Order of Battle: September 1980 78
Bibliography 78

List of Maps
Map 1: Khuzestan – The Iraqi invasion, September 1980 53
Map 2: Operations Hoveyzeh/Nasr, January 1981 53
Map 3: Operations Imam Ali (May 1981) and Tarigh al-Qods (November–December 1981) 54
Map 4: The Karun Bridgehead, June–September 1981 54
Map 5: Operation Beit ol Mogaddas, April May 1982 54

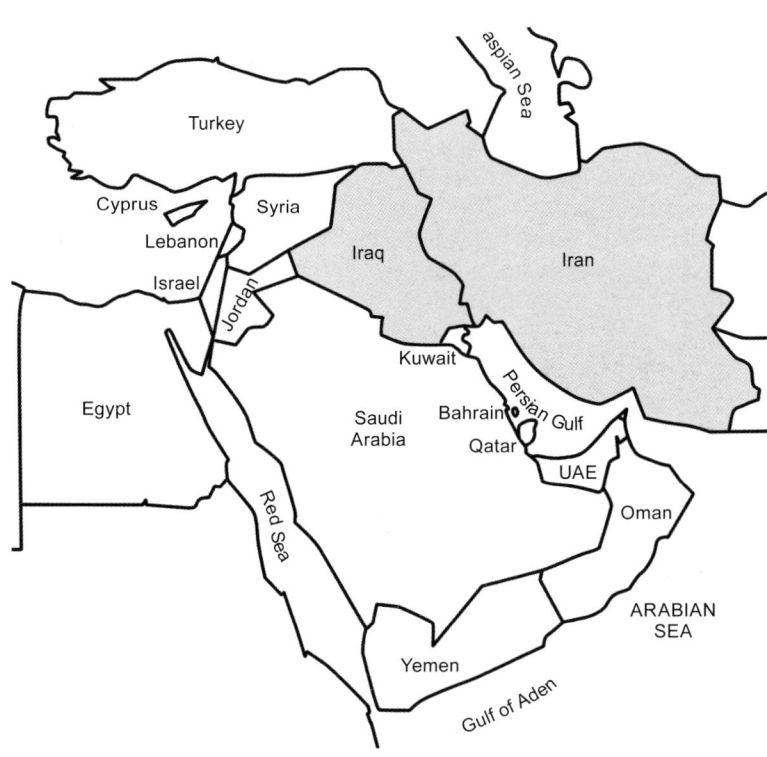

Helion & Company Limited
26 Willow Road
Solihull
West Midlands
B91 1UE
England
Tel. 0121 705 3393
Fax 0121 711 4075
Email: info@helion.co.uk
Website: www.helion.co.uk
Twitter: @helionbooks
Visit our blog http://blog.helion.co.uk/

Published by Helion & Company 2016
Designed and typeset by Kerrin Cocks, Publishing Services
Cover designed by Paul Hewitt, Battlefield Design (www.battlefield-design.co.uk)
Printed by Henry Ling, Dorchester, Dorset

Text © E. R. Hooton, Tom Cooper & Farzin Nadimi 2016
Images © as individually credited
Colour profiles © Tom Cooper & Radek Panchartek
Maps drawn by George Anderson © Helion & Company

ISBN 978-1-911096-56-6

British Library Cataloguing-in-Publication Data.
A catalogue record for this book is available from the British Library.

All rights reserved. No part of this publication may be reproduced, stored in a retrieval system, or transmitted, in any form, or by any means, electronic, mechanical, photocopying, recording or otherwise, without the express written consent of Helion & Company Limited.

For details of other military history titles published by Helion & Company Limited contact the above address, or visit our website: http://www.helion.co.uk.

We always welcome receiving book proposals from prospective authors.

Acknowledgements

I would like to thank Dr Kevin W. Woods, one of the leading researchers in the Iran-Iraq War, for his extremely useful advice in following certain lines of research, and Major General Aladdin Hussein Makki Khamas for his great kindness not only for taking time to respond to my queries from his encyclopedic knowledge of the Iraqi Army and the war with Iran, but also volunteering extra relevant information. He has done so with astonishing speed and with great courtesy, both of which I greatly appreciate.

I also want to thank Colonel Pesach Malovany, one of the leading non-Arab authorities on the Iraqi Army, for his assistance and advice. His comprehensive Hebrew-language history of the Iraqi Army, *Milhamot Bavel ha-Hadasha*, has been expanded and published in the English language and is one of the best foreign studies of this important army.

Finally my thanks also extend to my fellow writers Tom Cooper and Farzad Bishop, whose expertise on the Iran-Iraq War long predates my research into the subject. They have been a vital source of valuable information and corrected my most glaring errors despite their busy professional lives.

E.R. Hooton

Abbreviations

AFV	Armoured Fighting Vehicle.
APC	Armoured Personnel Carrier.
APDS	Armour-Piercing, Discarding Sabot. Anti-armour shell.
APFSDS	Armour-Piercing, Fin-Stabilised, Discarding Sabot. Anti-armour shel.1
ARV	Armoured Recovery Vehicle.
ATGM	Anti-Tank Guided Missile.
AVLB	Armoured Vehicle-Launched Bridge.
CAS	Close Air Support.
COIN	Counterinsurgency.
COMINT	Communications intelligence.
FEBA	Forward Edge of Battle Area.
Frog	ASCC acronym meaning Free Rocket Over Ground for 9K52 Luna (Moon) short range surface-to-surface missile.
Gainful	ASCC codename for 2K12 Kub (Cube) SAM, also designated SA-6.
Grail	ASCC codename for 9K32 Strela-2, Soviet MANPADS, also designated SA-7.
HAWK	Homing All-the-Way Killer. MIM-23 SAM.
HEAT	High Explosive Anti-Tank. Anti-armour shell.
HESH	High Explosive Squash Head. Anti-armour shell.
Hind	ASCC codename for Mil Mi-25 helicopter.
Hip	ASCC codename for Mil Mi-8 helicopter.
HOT	Haut subsonique Optiquement Télguide. Euromissile ATGM.
IFV	Infantry fighting vehicle.
IIG	Iranian Islamic Gendarmerie.
IrAAC	Iraqi Army Aviation Corps.
IrAF	Iraqi Air Force.
IRI	Islamic Republic of Iran.
IRIA	Islamic Republic of Iran Army.
IRIAA	Islamic Republic of Iran Army Aviation.
IRIAF	Islamic Republic of Iran Air Force.
MANPADS	Man-portable air defence system(s) – light surface-to-air missile system that can be carried and deployed in combat by a single soldier.
MBT	Main Battle Tank.
Mi	Mil (Soviet/Russian helicopter designer and manufacturer).
MiG	Mikoyan i Gurevich (the design bureau led by Artyom Ivanovich Mikoyan and Mikhail Iosifovich Gurevich, also known as OKB-155 or MMZ 'Zenit').
MLR	Main Line of Resistance.
Pasdaran	Iranian Revolutionary Guards Corps.
POW	Prisoner of War.
RCC	Revolutionary Command Council.
RPG	Rocket-Propelled Grenade.
SAM	Surface-to-Air Missile.
Scud	ASCC codename for R-17 Elbrus surface-to-surface missile, also called SS-1.
SFOH	Southern Forward Operations Headquarters (Iranian).
SIGINT	Signals intelligence.
Swatter	ASCC codename for 3M11 or Fleyta (Flute) (AT-2A Swatter A).and 9K17 or Skorpion (Scorpion) (AT-2B Swatter B) ATGM.
TOW	Tube-launched Optically tracked Wire-guided ATGM, officially designated BGM-71.
USSR	Union of Soviet Socialist Republics (or Soviet Union).

1
Background to a Bloody War

For 94 months between 1980 and 1988, Iran and Iraq fought the longest, uninterrupted, conventional conflict of the twentieth century, which cost hundreds of thousands of lives. It was called The Imposed War by the Iranians, the Great Qadisiyya or Qadisiyyat Saddam by the Iraqis, or simply the Gulf War, until that term was press-ganged to describe Iraq's 19901991 and 2003 conflicts with the American-led Coalition.[1]

The conflict may be the last 'conventional war' which involved masses of men and equipment in a direct struggle, and the cost was huge. Western post-war studies usually calculate Iraqi casualties at 190,0001,040,000, including 150,000340,000 killed, with another 70,000 POWs, and Iranian casualties at 1,050,0001,930,000, including 450,000730,000 killed, while 45,000 were taken prisoner.[2]. Such figures are much inflated, for official Iranian publications are citing 1,133,000 casualties, including 188,000 dead and 945,000 wounded, with 73,000 missing military personnel. Not usually involved in such reports are about 90,000 civilian casualties, including 11,000 dead. In comparison, no official data on Iraqi casualties was ever released.[3] Furthermore, the conflict caused about 2.5 million refugees and cost $228 billion, of which $3240 billion was spent on weapons.[4]

The region is one of the Middle East's cockpits because the Tigris-Euphrates plain, which forms the heartland of Iraq, has long been a cultural watershed. It marked the fiercely contested eastern boundary of the Roman, Arab and Ottoman Empires against the Parthians and Persians, as well as the fault line in the Islamic schism between Sunni and Shi'a. Modern Iran and Iraq were born as monarchies after the First World War, with growing oil wealth, but both were occupied by the Allied Powers during the Second World War. In the post-war world, each sought to buttress its independence from external pressure, but followed very different routes which laid the foundations for this war.[5]

Centuries of the Ottoman Empire and decades of quasi-colonial rule of the British and French over territories predominantly populated by Arabs and Moslems in the Middle East, and the creation of a number of artificial nations (including Lebanon, Syria, Iraq, Jordan and Palestine) with arbitrary borders instead of a unified Arab state widely demanded by the local population, resulted in the spread of pan-Arab nationalism and anti-imperialism during the 1950s. However, the rule of the major protagonist of such ideas, Egyptian President Gamal Abdel Nasser, disappointed many and created plenty of unrest, especially in Iraq and Syria. Amid latent political instability that spread through the Middle East during the early 1960s, and in the light of the creation of Israel in 19471949, a number of newly emerging Arab leaders usurped the ideology of radical change along the ideals of the Arab Socialist Renaissance Party (al-Ba'ath al-Arabi al-Ishtiraki, colloquially the Ba'ath Party). Ba'ath regimes established their control over Iraq and Syria: while stabilizing the political situation and resulting in a period of unprecedented economic growth, they maintained themselves in power with the help of police states.

Mohammed Reza Shah Pahlavi, ruler of Iran from 1943, regarded Moscow as the prime threat to his regme and placed himself firmly on the Western side during the Cold War. He exploited Iran's geopolitical location to strengthen its position both within the Persian Gulf (called the Arabian Gulf by his Arab neighbours) and south-west Asia, while also seeking to modernise the country's economy and social structure. Neighbouring Iraq was his closest rival; their relations were marred by economic rivalry and religious friction, because most Iranian

Abadan refinery at the time one of the largest in the world in the 1940s, with the Shatt al-Arab in the right foreground. (Mark Lepko Collection)

The first indication of new relations between Iran and the USA occurred in 1967, when Tehran was granted permission to place an order for 32 McDonnell Douglas F-4D Phantom II interceptors. Ten years later, nearly 230 Phantom IIs of three major variants formed the backbone of the Iranian Air Force. (Tom Cooper Collection)

Shah Mohammad Reza Pahlavi, Emperor of Iran and a close US ally for nearly 30 years, played an influential role in pushing through a number of spectacular arms deals that brought the latest US technology to his country in the 1970s. (Mark Lepko Collection)

After spending more than 15 years in exile for his opposition to the Shah, Grand Ayatollah Seyed Ruhollah Musavi Khomeini (known in the West as Ayatollah Khomeini) became the Supreme Leader of the Islamic Republic of Iran the new highest-ranking political and religious authority of the nation. (Mark Lepko Collection)

Saddam Hussein Abd al-Majid at-Tikriti played a key role in the 1968 coup (also known as the 17th July Revolution) that brought the Ba'ath Party to power in Iraq, and installed himself as the fifth president of the country in July 1979. (Mark Lepko Collection)

Moslems are Shi'a, as well as the Shah's unofficial support for Israel. With the decline of British power in the early 1970s, and emboldened by the administration of US President Richard B. Nixon, the Shah of Iran sought to become the dominant military and political power in the Middle East. Sending a clear signal to all neighbours, in November 1971, only a day after the official British withdrawal from the Persian Gulf, the Iranian military seized the Abu Mussa and Tunb Islands in the Hormuz Straits. Although held by Persians for most of the last few thousand years, these strategically positioned islands were meanwhile claimed by the United Arab Emirates (UAE), another British artificial creation, combing six minor sheikhdoms into a federation that was developed into a major financial powerhouse in the area.

Exploiting military links between Baghdad and Moscow for his purposes, the Shah then sought to undermine the Ba'ath regime in Iraq by supporting Kurdish tribesmen in the north of that country. At odds with successive Iraqi governments since the country's creation, the Kurds launched a major uprising that sucked 160,000 of the Iraqi Army's 200,000 men into a campaign waged through most of 1974 and into early 1975. The then Foreign Minister of the Iraqi government, but already the actual strongman in Baghdad, Saddam Hussein al-Takriti (usually known as Saddam) would later claim this war cost Iraq up to 17,000 casualties and most of the national military's ammunition stocks.[6]

Eventually, the governments in Baghdad and Tehran accepted an Algerian-brokered agreement on 6 March 1975. Like many Iraqis, Saddam regarded it as a personal humiliation, for the terms were dictated by Tehran – meanwhile further emboldened by immense purchases of arms from the USA. Iran ceased military support for the Kurds but would now share in control of the Shatt al-Arab (the Shatt), called the River Arvand by the Iranians, the waterway between the two states. Baghdad had always claimed exclusive authority over the Shatt, which leads to Iraq's main port of Basra and the major Iranian ports of Khorramshahr and Abadan. The agreement also called upon both countries to formally define their land frontier, which Iraq interpreted as Tehran's willingness to cede some 240km² of disputed border territory around Qasr-e Shirin and Mehran.

The Iranians sent a delegation to Baghdad, which led to the Treaty on International Borders and Good Neighbourly Relations on 13 June 1975, known as the Algiers Treaty as it was brokered by the Algerians and signed in their capital, yet within three days Iraq sought to improve its terms at bayonet point. The army threw a pontoon bridge across the Shatt and used it to establish a bridgehead in Khuzestan, but the Iranians crushed the incursion within two days after 88 Iraqis and three Iranians were killed.[7] While railing against the new 'imperialists', Baghdad could do little as Tehran now dominated the region, boosted by its economic and demographic power. Iran produced 5.2 million barrels of oil per day in 1978, compared with Iraq's 2.6 million, and had more than 39 million people, of whom 5.1 million men could serve in the armed forces; this compared with an Iraqi population of 13.5 million, of whom only 1.7 million could be called to the colours.[8]

In the uneasy peace which followed the Algiers Treaty, the Shah used the vast wealth created by the 1973 1974 oil crisis to further strengthen and modernize his military forces and industry, spending about $15.5 billion on equipment between 1975 and 1979 (compared with Iraq's $8.1 billion).[9] The Ba'ath Party regime in Baghdad also faced a problem with the Shi'a, who made up 50 65 percent of the population and were increasingly restive under Sunni rule. Many Iraqi Ba'athists feared that Tehran might encourage an uprising of the Shi'a. Saddam's cousin and mentor, President Ahmad Hassan al-Bakr, reportedly sought a conciliatory approach, but hardliners led by Saddam engineered his overthrow in July 1979: they replaced him as president and began to persecute both the Shi'a and communists.[10]

A regime change with tremendous consequences for the entire Middle East then took place in Iran. The Shah's efforts to modernize the country and its military were compromised by the end of the oil boom and declining oil prices. This further exacerbated already high social divisions in the country, and resulted in mass protesting through 1978. Already facing massive criticism for often brutal methods of ruling his country, the Mohammed Reza Shah Pahlavi was surprised by the protests and determined to use troops to suppress the unrest. But the armed forces, although personally dominated by the Shah, were reluctant to confront civilian unrest and lacked the training for this role. Except for a few lukewarm attempts to quash protests, the most notorious of which resulted in 'Black Friday' on 8 September

The Iranian order for 80 Grumman F-14A Tomcat interceptors and associated AIM-54A Phoenix long-range air-to-air missiles, placed in 19731974, was another high point of US-Iranian relations of that time. (Tom Cooper Collection)

1978, before long elements of the military began joining the masses, making the country de-facto ungovernable.

In times of trouble, people tend to turn to God. While much of this mass protest movement was organized and run by very different political parties, religion began to play an ever more important role. Always strongly influenced by their religious leaders (ayatollahs, imans and mullahs), the urban and rural poor joined the calls for the replacement of the Shah's secular regime with one based upon Islamic spiritual values. On 16 January 1979, Mohammed Reza Shah Pahlavi felt forced to leave the country: he went into exile in the USA and then Egypt, where he would die in July 1980.[11]

Meanwhile, on 1 February 1979, the spiritual leader of Iranian Shi'a, Ayatollah Ruhollah al-Musavi al-Khomeini, returned from years of exile to a tumultuous reception of over a million in Tehran. In the course of a fierce power struggle during the following months of this Islamic Revolution – some of which included fire-fights between members of different Iranian political parties – Khomeni established himself in power over the theocratic, Islamic Republic of Iran (IRI), aiming to create 'God's Kingdom on Earth' in the form of an 'Islamic imamate'.[12]

For any opponents of the new rule – whether active, or even only suspected – the newly declared IRI became a literal 'hell on earth'. Those seeking greater secular power or demanding regional autonomy faced widespread arrests, endless brutalities and summary executions. Unsurprisingly, some – especially Kurds in north-western Iran – responded by launching insurgencies, while others reacted with terrorism.

Inevitably, the revolutionary fervour crossed the border to Iraq, which soon harboured many opponents of the clerics, while within Iraq's Shi'a community a militant organization, the al-Daawa al-Ismaliya (Islamic Call or Daawa) party, began a terror campaign. Their spiritual leader, Ayatollah Muhammad Baqer al-Sadr, was a personal friend of Khomeini and pointedly noted that 'other tyrants' would see their day of reckoning. Shi'a pro-Khomeini demonstrations in June 1979 led to a crackdown with numerous arrests. On 30 March 1980, Baghdad made membership of Daawa a capital offence, while the following day, the party tried unsuccessfully to assassinate Iraq's Foreign Minister and Deputy Premier Tariq Aziz, which led Saddam in retaliation to execute al-Sadr.[13]

Opponents of the Iraqi and Iranian regimes traditionally found sanctuary across the border indeed Khomeini had been expelled from Iraq following the Algiers Treaty so naturally each side accused the other of supporting their opponents. Saddam hoped the new regime in Tehran would be more flexible on the land-border provisions of the Algiers Treaty, but the revolutionary regime focused upon internal threats, despite small-scale border clashes which began even as Saddam assumed power. On 31 October 1979, Saddam set out his stall when he publicly demanded the abrogation of the Algiers Treaty, the restoration of 'Iraqi rights' over the Shatt, the evacuation of Abu Musa and the Tunbs, as well as full autonomy both to Iran's Kurds of Kordestan Province and the Sunni Arabs of Khuzestan Province which borders the Shatt. Tehran naturally rejected these demands and tensions rose steadily. Then on 6 November 1979, two days after the US Embassy in Tehran was occupied and its staff taken hostage, Iraqi consulate offices in Kermanshah and Khorramshahr were seized. In March 1980, Iraq and Iran expelled each other's ambassadors and the diplomatic war escalated, although they did not formally break off diplomatic relations until June that year. This followed Iraq's first elections since the monarchy was overthrown in 1958 which led to a Ba'athist majority, which strengthened Saddam's control over the country while providing a veneer of popular support.

Although some Western observers recently concluded that Saddam's decision to invade Iran was de facto a 'snap-shot' reaction, taken in a matter of only two days, it was actually a well thought-out action. Beginning to regard himself as a new Salahaddin (the Tikrit-born An-Nasir Salah ad-Din Yusuf iby Ayyub, better known in the West as Saladin), Saddam intended to exploit his country's economic and military power to lead a renaissance in which he would restore the Arabs to a leading role on the world stage.[14] By the early summer of 1980, Egypt's political accommodation with Israel had undermined that country's prestige in the Arab world, Jordan was Iraq's traditional friend, while negotiations for a union with Syria failed. This left Iran, Baghdad's traditional foe, as an obstacle to Saddam's ambitions and one which now sought to undermine his regime. With this arch enemy – and especially its military – in a state of chaos, there was a unique opportunity for Iraq to exploit the situation. This becomes obvious when studying such Iraqi documents as a report from the General Military Intelligence Directorate (Mudiriyyat al-Istikhabarat al-Askariyya al-Amma, GMID) on the state of Iran during the first half of 1980, issued in July of that year.[15] This noted the country was racked by internecine fighting as the economy collapsed, aggravated by Khomeini's ill health and imminent 'departure', which was envisaged within the next two years. The report played into Saddam's hands, 'confirming' it was time for the Iraqi military to make a show

Nowadays colloquially known as the Islamic Revolution, public unrest in Iran in 1978 and 1979 was originally organized by a number of diverse groups, including not only Islamists but several leftist political parties. (Albert Grandolini Collection)

A view of downtown Baghdad, the capital of the Republic of Iraq, with Jamahiriya Bridge, in the mid-1970s, when the city was the epicentre of a rapidly developing nation. (Mark Lepko Collection)

of force along the border, suck in the remaining meagre Iranian military resources and thus accelerate regime change in Tehran.

This decision was communicated at a joint meeting of the Ba'ath Party and State Command on 6 July at Abu Ghraib, 32km west of Baghdad, although Saddam, together with Iraqi Air Force (IrAF), Air Defence and Navy commanders were absent.[16] Attending this meeting were Defence Minister General Adnan Khairallah Talfah (usually referred to as Khairallah), Army chief-of-staff General Jabbah al-Shanshal and Operations chief Lieutenant General Abdul al-Jabar al-Asadi.[17] The following day, corps and divisional commanders were informed Saddam intended to invade Iran to pre-empt an Iranian attack, which would encourage Shi'a rebel activity. According to Lieutenant General Ra'ad Majid Rashid al-Hamdani, many of these military leaders were convinced war was inevitable due to 'Iran's continuous attacks'. It was later claimed that while all the corps and divisional commanders regarded war as inevitable, none were enthusiastic, but, according to Major General Aladdin Hussein Makki Khamas, only the 7th Infantry Division (Inf Div) commander, Brigadier Nayar al-Kharyranyi (al-Khazraji), raised serious concerns about the operation's prospects. He noted the army had focused upon counter-insurgency for the best part of a decade and would take two years to regain proficiency in conventional operations. The others, fearing Saddam's wrath, reprimanded him for openly expressing such pessimism, although it is likely that most shared these very justified concerns.

Shanshal was assigned the task of planning operations, but although described as a good staff officer and instructor he was also said to be a bad military leader with a '1940s mentality', while the British Defence Attaché to Baghdad noted in 1981 that he had served for 10 years and 'he is getting older and fatter'.[18] He sensibly delegated the task to Asadi, a British staff school graduate regarded as 'an excellent officer'.[19] Asadi did not, as some claimed, simply rewrite a British staff exercise in the Baghdad War College or the 1941 Anglo-Indian Army invasion of Persia.[20] The Iraqis had long prepared cross-border contingency plans, which focused upon seizing the main communications hubs in western Iran together with the Bytaq and Dezful passes in the Zagros Mountains.[21] The growing strength of the Iranian Army forced major revisions of these plans during Bakr's presidency. The objective now was simply to occupy Khuzestan, which had a large ethnic Arab population and was more accessible to mechanized forces, while its oil wealth made it a valuable strategic asset.

Asadi retained this element for Operation Qadisiyya II, but adjusted it to meet Saddam's political aims, which resembled those of Egypt's President Gamal Abdel Nasser when he ordered his military to deploy in the Sinai in May 1967: as a game of political chess. Saddam aimed to force Tehran to renegotiate the Algiers Treaty in Iraq's favour by seizing territory as a bargaining counter. Asadi's plan reflected this and envisaged a four-to-six-week operation in which light forces would first cross the border and penetrate some 5km to detect, locate and reduce enemy reserves. The heavy, mechanized forces would then advance 10–20km into Iran in what have been described as 'tank raids', with each division given a city or major town as an objective. Saddam anticipated the Iranians would strip troops from the interior to stop the invaders; this would weaken resistance to popular uprisings, which would establish a secular government more compliant to Iraqi demands. The plan's great flaw was the assumption the new government would be more compliant; it ignored profound Iranian nationalism.[22]

Saddam's timing of the offensive would have ominous echoes of Operation Barbarossa, Hitler's invasion of Russia in 1941, where the Wehrmacht's initial success was followed by stubborn and bitter resistance which caused it to be stopped by the harsh Russian winter. Saddam's timing was undoubtedly driven by meteorological conditions, for summer temperatures in Khuzestan, the prime theatre, can reach 45–50°C.[23] However, during the winter, the major rivers are swollen by rain and water from the mountains, while in the north, the troops would also face ice and snow. Iraqi planners may have foreseen the weather as an ally to hamstring the Iranian response, but only if Baghdad's troops achieved all their objectives before the weather turned, rather like Hitler and Moscow in October 1941. From late September, the temperature drops to around 35–40°C, but there is only a narrow window of opportunity before the winter rains turn desert into marshland and confine all movement to roads on embankments. Between June and September, there is virtually no rain in western Khuzestan, but the monthly total in the Ahvaz-Abadan area, in which Ahvaz receives approximately 33 percent of the rainfall, shows 5.7mm in October, 26.15mm in November, 41.65mm in December and 43.8mm in January. The rainfall gradually eases into March.[24]

Chapter 1 Notes
1. During the Battle of Qadisiyya (or Qadisiyyah or Qadeisiyya) in November 636, the Arabs defeated a Sassanid Persian army, marking the beginning of the end of Persian rule in Iraq and of the Persian Empire. Hiro, p.44.

In an effort to match the US-Iranian partnership, Iraq signed several friendship and trade treaties with Moscow during the 1970s. Among others, these resulted in delivery of Mikoyan i Gurevich MiG-23MS interceptors to the IrAF. Iraqi expectations for this type were greatly disappointed, because it proved no match for the US-made F-14As acquired by Iran. (Farzin Nadimi Collection)

Hardened by the years-long war against the Kurds and especially the October 1973 War with Israel, and equipped with reasonably advanced fighter-bombers of Soviet origin, IrAF pilots considered themselves the elite of the Iraqi military. This is a group of fliers from the No. 5 or No. 44 Squadron in front of a Sukhoi Su-20M (serial number 2077), in the summer of 1980. (Tom Cooper Collection)

2. Cordesman et al, pp.23.
3. See H.W.Beuttel's articles in the TNDM newsletter.
4. *Lessons*, pp.23; *Jane's Defence Weekly*, 'The international arms industry: Final casualty of the Gulf War', 30 July 1988.
5. The background to the Gulf War is sketched out in O'Ballance, *The Gulf War*, pp.129, hereafter O'Ballance. *Lessons*, pp.1039. There are numerous works which provide greater detail.
6. Conflict Record Research Center (CRRC) SH–SHTP-A-000-835. See also Al-Marashi and Salama, *Iraq's Armed Forces*, hereafter Marashi & Salama, pp.12122; Cooper & Bishop, *Iran-Iraq War in the Air*, pp.6163, hereafter Cooper & Bishop; Farrokh, *Iran at War*, pp.31317, hereafter Farrokh; Pollack, *Arabs at War*, pp.17682, herafter Pollack, *Arabs*; Ward, *Immortal: A military history of Iran and its armed Forces*, p.203, hereafter Ward. UK Defence Attache's Annual Report 1981, UK National Archives (UK NA) FCO 8/4156. Strictly, the Iraqi leader should be referred to as Hussein, but the West's more common use of his personal name will be retained in this narrative.
7. Cooper & Bishop, p.62; Farrokh, pp.31317.
8. *Lessons*, pp.54, 91.
9. Op cit, p.22.
10. Saddam was a civilian, despite his military titles. He was also chairman of the supreme decision-making body, the Revolutionary Command Council (RCC).
11. Khomeini is also transliterated as Khomeyni.
12. Murray & Woods, *The Iran-Iraq War*, pp.3839, 44, hereafter Murray & Woods.
13. Op cit, p.44.
14. Similar views shaped his decision to invade Kuwait in 1990.
15. CRRC SH-GMD-D-000-842.
16. The town would become infamous due to the American treatment of prisoners in the jail.
17. For the Iraqi Army and the decision to go to war, see Woods et al, *Project 1946*, pp.4849, hereafter *Project 1946*. This is qualified by Woods et al, *Saddam's War: An Iraqi Military Perspective Of The Iran-Iraq War*, pp.2729, hereafter *Saddam's War*, and *Saddam's Generals: Perspectives of the Iran-Iraq War*, pp.55, 11516, hereafter *Saddam's Generals*; Murray & Woods, p.47.
18. Comment by Lieutenant General Aladdin Hussein Makki Khamas and in UKNA FCO 8/4156. See also Murray & Woods, p.64 f/n 52.
19. *Saddam's Generals*, pp.53, 113.
20. This suggestion was first made by US journalist R. Halloran, 'British in 1950, Helped Map Iraqi Invasion of Iran', in the *New York Times*, 16 October 1980. Farrokh, p.347; O'Ballance, p.48.
21. For planning, see Malovany Milhamot Bavel ha-Hadasha, *The Wars of Modern Babylon*, pp.10912, 11617, hereafter Malovany; *Saddam's Generals*, pp.12830; *Saddam's War*, pp.5455, 113, 11516.
22. *Saddam's Generals*, pp.52, 5657.
23. All weather data is based upon the Kuwait weather forecast, Weather History, daily archive in the Freemeteo website and Kuwait archive for the period 19801988.
24 Based upon websites Climatological Normals of Abadan and Ahwaz Climate Climate of Ahwaz Iran/world climate.

2
Two Armies

While nominally an instrument of national foreign policy, the Iraqi military was primarily an internal security force.[1] During the Arab-Israeli Wars of 19481949, in June 1967 and in October 1973, the Iraqi Republic despatched its military forces against Israel, but Israeli and most Western reporting usually rates their performance as the 'worst of all Arab forces'.[2] However, official and unofficial Iraqi sources stress the Iraqi Air Force (IrAF) fared much better than usually assessed.

The losses the Iraqi Army suffered during the October 1973 war were quickly replaced by rapid purchases from Czechoslovakia and the Soviet Union, which included about 800 T-54/55, 1,300 T-62 and 155 T-72 main battle tanks (MBT), 1,600 BTR-60/BTR-152 wheeled and 200 BTR-50 tracked armoured personnel carriers (APC), as well as 620 BMP tracked infantry fighting vehicles (IFV), by 1980. Substantial quantities of artillery were also supplied to give Iraq 900 guns, including 126 D-30 122mm howitzers, 60 D-74 122mm guns, 400 M-46 130mm guns, 96 ML-20, 75 D-20 and 36 D-1 152mm howitzers, and nine S-23 180mm guns, supported by 90 Multiple Launch Rocket Launchers (MLRS) 36 BM-21s and 54 BM-13s.[3]

Impressed by US-made M109 and M110 self-propelled howitzers imported by Iran, Baghdad sought similar equipment and in 1978 placed orders for 50 2S1 Gvozdika (Carnation) 122mm self-propelled howitzers and 50 2S3 Akatsiya (Acacia) 152mm self-propelled guns. Only two batteries of these were in service with the 6th Armoured

Division (Arm Div) by 1980, but none saw service before 1982.[4]. Other equipment was purchased from Czechoslovakia, including 395 OT-62 Topas tracked APCs with 70 ambulance versions, and 386 OT-64 SKOT wheeled APCs, most of which were delivered, but negotiations for 100 T-54A tanks (T-55M) apparently failed.[5] Overall, Ba'athist relations with the Soviet Union and its allies were always stormy, and thus Soviet advisors were never permitted to work with Iraqi military units.

Baghdad also sought to find alternative sources of arms. Following lengthy negotiations with Paris, Iraq contracted Panhard for 185 AML-60/90 reconnaissance vehicles, 205 M-3 light wheeled APCs and 100 ERC-TH anti-armour missile vehicles in 1968. In the mid-1970s, orders were also placed for French aircraft and missiles.[6] The Iraqi Army also purchased 200 Engesa EE-9 Cascavel reconnaissance vehicles from Brazil, with deliveries beginning in 1979.[7] The strategic movement of heavy armour would be aided by the expansion of the tank transporter fleet from 205 West German Fauns in 1973 to about 1,000 in 1986.[8]

This equipment meant that by 1980, Baghdad had momentarily achieved military equality, if not superiority, with Iran, fielding an army of some 200,000 plus 256,000 reservists, supported by about 2,600 tanks, a similar number of APCs and IFVs, and 800 artillery pieces.[9] This equipment was operated by 12 divisions controlled by three corps headquarters, and six independent manoeuvre brigades. Another independent brigade was assigned to the Navy, while two missile brigades were operating Soviet-made 9K52 Luna-M (ASCC-code FROG-7) and R-17E (ASCC-code SS-1 Scud) surface-to-surface missiles.

The three corps commands and their divisions were distributed as follows:

I Corps with headquarters in Kirkuk, in control over 2nd, 4th and 7th Mountain Divisions (Mtn Div), the 8th and reinforced 11th Inf Divs, 12th Arm Div and 31st and 32nd Special Forces Brigades (SF Bdes). The corps had a total of 21 manoeuvre brigades, which were smaller than their IRIA equivalents.

II Corps controlled the strategic reserve and was headquartered in Baghdad. It controlled the 3rd, 6th and 10th Arm Divs with a total of 11 manoeuvre brigades; the 10th Armoured Brigade (Arm Bde) and the 17th SF Brig. The 10th Arm Bde supported the Republican Guards Brigade (Al-Haris al-Jamhuri), which consisted of four manoeuvre battalions, and was further augmented by elements of 31st SF Brig.

III Corps was headquartered in Nassiriyah. It controlled the 1st and 5th Mechanized Divisions (Mech Divs) and 9th Arm Div, including a total of 10 manoeuvre brigades.[10]

The Iraqi Army exercised control over the Border Guard Force with a nominal 24 brigades, which was transferred to the Defence Ministry on 4 February 1980 to support the army in counter-insurgency operations, although it would also augment the regular army on the southern front.[11]

A reserve was created from 1974 based upon 10 regional administrative brigades, each with six battalions, loosely supported by regular infantry divisions.[12] There was also the Ba'ath Party's paramilitary organization to counter-balance the army, the Popular Army

Some of the first modern armoured vehicles of the Imperial Iranian Army were US-made M24 Chafee light tanks, one of which is on this photo from the early 1970s. By 1980, they had been replaced by the British-made Scorpions, and were instead used as static pillboxes along the border with Iraq. (Albert Grandolini Collection)

The Chieftain was the backbone of the Iranian armoured formations, especially six battalions assigned to the 92nd Armoured Division deployed in Khuzestan, close to the Iraqi border. Other units equipped with the type included the 16th and 81st Armoured Divisions, and the 37th Armoured Brigade, while the 88th Brigade was in the process of preparing to convert to much more advanced Shir Iran MBTs when the Shah was toppled. (Tom Cooper Collection)

In the early 1970s, Iran acquired 460 M60A1s. The type was assigned to mechanized battalions of infantry divisions, but also to eight tank battalions of the 81st Armoured Division (deployed in north-western Iran). (Albert Grandolini Collection)

The oldest main battle tank type still in active service with the Iranian Army in 1980 were survivors of 400 M47 tanks acquired in the late 1960s, and then locally upgraded (primarily through installation of new engines) to M47M standard. Each Iranian division boasted two battalions equipped with M47Ms. (Albert Grandolini Collection)

(Al-Jaysh Al- Shabi), which had 75,000 men under Taha Yasin Ramadan al-Jazrawi and whose Chief-of-Staff was Brigadier General Ghazi Mahmud al-Omar Saddam. It was created on 8 February 1970 under the Revolutionary Command Council (RCC) as the successor of the National Guard to give Party members military training and provided an excuse for them to dress like soldiers. All Ba'ath Party members aged 18–45 were given compulsory training, nominally for six hours a week, to handle small arms, while units attended an annual camp during the summer to receive some rudimentary combat training. It was steadily expanded from 50,000 in 1975, and by 1980 the leadership was seeking Cuban assistance to triple its size.[13]

The focus of Iraqi training was on conventional operations against Israel or Iran. The Iraqi military drew many important lessons from its involvement in the June 1967 and October 1973 Arab-Israeli Wars, and during the 1970s undertook serious attempts to improve professional standards within the officer corps and a great effort to provide realistic combined arms tactical training for conventional warfare.[14] To some degree, training was hindered by overdependence on conscripts, many of whom were illiterate. Overall, while the Army managed to run several combined arms exercises, most of the training of its different elements was undertaken in isolation.[15]

This issue proved a handicap during counter-insurgency (COIN) operations against the Kurds which had involved I Corps, Special Forces and brigades rotated or drafted into Kurdistan. The guerrilla war against the Kurds diluted Iraqi Army training in conventional warfare, despite clashes with the Imperial Iranian Army (Artesh Rahaibakhshe Iran). Even five years later, lack of expertise had not been overcome: in late 1980, a staff officer was forced to inform Saddam that an entire brigade never received any kind of training on a weapons system as simple as the Soviet-made RPG-7, which was in widespread use.[16]

The Iraqi Air Force was a proud service and theoretically a significant asset, with at least 330 combat aircraft. It could look back to a long history and rich heritage, as well as a number of battles against Israel. However, it was primarily equipped for air defence purposes and COIN warfare against the Kurds, and its offensive capabilities were minimal.

Another major problem was the politicisation of senior command. In July 1979, Saddam removed all the corps and division commanders, many of whom were well-regarded professionally, and replaced them

One of the the Shah's final decision before he was forced to leave the country was to deploy his army against protesters. This Chieftain broke down and was then abandoned by its crew. (Albert Grandolini Collection)

In 1979–1980, the remaining Iranian M47Ms were largely replaced by M48s and M60s, and frequently operated on internal security duties. This example was photographed on the streets of Tehran in January 1979. (Albert Grandolini Collection)

with men loyal to him. Many were junior officers, few of whom had commanded even a brigade, while fewer were qualified staff officers. The nominal supreme decision-making body, the RCC, had no professional military leaders. Saddam himself received an honorary degree from Iraq's military college in 1976 and was given the rank of lieutenant general, and three years later as president and commander-in-chief he was 'promoted' to field marshal. His brother-in-law,

Although the Shah's military did open fire on several occasions, most of its troops eventually sided with protesters as did the crew of this Scorpion reconnaissance tank and several other soldiers. (Albert Grandolini Collection)

During the 1970s, the Iranian Army experimented a lot with various heavy equipment and the organization of its large units, and was thus relatively slow in purchasing self-propelled artillery. Correspondingly, only about 430 155mm M109A1 self-propelled howitzers were acquired. (Albert Grandolini Collection)

Although a staunch US ally, the Shah and the Iranian military also ordered Soviet-made arms whenever Washington showed reluctance to deliver whatever the Iranians thought was necessary for them to buy. One such contract with Moscow from 1969 resulted in the delivery of BTR-60 armoured personnel carriers. This example was guarding an official building in Tehran in early 1979. (Albert Grandolini Collection)

Khairallah, was a junior officer rapidly promoted first to colonel and then to general in October 1977, before becoming Defence Minister. To control the Army throughout the war, Saddam would rule through a 'carrot and stick' (in Arabic targhib/tarhib) policy. The former meant promotions, pay rises and generous fringe benefits, while the latter involved constant monitoring of the Army by the security apparatus, which could arrest or rotate anyone at Saddam's will.[17] Ultimate decision-making was in Saddam's hands and he allowed his subordinates little initiative, so they would respond to crises by seeking his orders.

At the time of the Shah's fall, the Imperial Iranian Army, soon renamed the Islamic Republic of Iran Army (IRIA), was nominally the most powerful in the Middle East, capable of meeting and at least delaying even a Soviet mechanized threat. Many of its officers and non-commissioned officers (NCOs) had fresh combat experience from Oman, where six brigades with air support had been rotated on three-month tours since the early 1970s to help the Sultan against Communist-motivated insurgents active in Dhofar Province. A British general who served with them noted the leadership still seemed to be feudally based, with an emphasis upon obedience to authority rather than initiative.[18] However, there is meanwhile little doubt that Iranian involvement in this conflict proved instrumental for one of only the few completely successful COIN efforts in the history of modern warfare. Other problems reported by American advisors included a tendency to rely upon firepower rather than manoeuvre, as well as shortages of NCOs, training and storage facilities. Finally, the Shah's constant reshuffles of commanders – aimed to thwart the prospects of any kind of military coups – also caused many problems.[19]

With up to 30 percent of national revenues spent upon the armed forces, the Army was lavishly equipped, especially by the United States, which sold it $16 billion worth of equipment between 1972 and 1977, ostensibly to balance Iraqi acquisitions but actually to ensure a reliable US ally dominated the Gulf.[20] Here it is worth mentioning that while the Imperial Iranian Army was purchasing much equipment, many of these sophisticated acquisitions proved difficult to assimilate, as the Army spent most of the 1970s trying to reorganize and modernize itself based upon US experience in South-East Asia and Israeli lessons from the Holy Day War. Furthermore, a combination of large-scale acquisitions of most modern equipment and rapid expansion of the force resulted in lack of qualified and experienced personnel, leaving Tehran heavily dependent upon large numbers of foreign advisors and even technical support, despite immense investment into support infrastructure and large-scale development of the domestic defence sector.

During the late 1960s and through the 1970s, Iran acquired some 300 M47M, 150 M48A5 and 460 M60A1 MBTs for tank battalions assigned to infantry divisions. Mechanized and Reconnaissance battalions were equipped with about 300 M113A1/A2 tracked APCs, more than 500 self-propelled (430 M109A1 155mm, 38 M107 175mm, 38 M110 203mm guns) and 450 towed artillery pieces (330 M101 105mm, 112 M114 155mm and 14 M115 203mm howitzers). The towed artillery was usually assigned to infantry formations, while self-propelled artillery pieces were assigned to armoured formations and independent artillery groups, the latter each having four or five battalions and a MLRS battalion.[21]

During the Shah's rule, the government in Tehran also sought other sources for equipment, notably the United Kingdom, which supplied Scorpion tracked reconnaissance vehicles. More importantly, in December 1971, London and Tehran signed a contract worth £654 million for nearly 800 Chieftain AFVs, including 750 FV 4201 MBTs, 73 FV 4204 Armoured Recovery Vehicles (ARV) and 14 FV 4205 armoured bridge layers (AVLB). Three years later, the British received a £1.2 billion contract for development and procurement

As well as M109s, Iran also acquired 38 203mm M110 self-propelled howitzers. With their range of 32km, they could out-gun any artillery in the Iraqi arsenal. Iranian self-propelled artillery was assigned to mechanized and reconnaissance battalions, and proved undoubtedly superior to its Iraqi opponents. (Albert Grandolini Collection)

Another Iranian order for Soviet arms from 1969 resulted in the delivery of 100 ZSU-23-4 Shilka quadruple, radar-guided, self-propelled anti-aircraft guns. (Albert Grandolini Collection)

of 1,475 MBTs under the three-phase FV 4030 programme: this included deliveries of 150 improved Chieftains (FV 4030/1), 125 redesigned Chieftains (FV 4030/2) designated Shir or Shir Iran 1, and 1,200 redesigned Chieftains with Chobham armour (FV 4030/3) as Shir or Shir Iran 2. This contract was modified, with the last 43 MBTs of the original order being added to the FV 4030/1 contract.[22]

Between 1973 and 1978, Iran purchased 707 MBTs (73 Mk 3/3P and 624 Mk 5/3P), 14 AVLBs (1975 1976) and 41 ARVs (1978 1979). From the FV 4030 programme, Iran received only 185 MBTs (Mk 5/5P): two MBTs were retained in Britain for trials and demonstrations while six were in the process of being re-engined when Tehran cancelled this order, plus that for 77 further Chieftains (including eight FV 4030/1 and 32 ARVs), in February 1979.[23] The Chieftains equipped 15 tank battalions in the 16th and 92nd Arm Divs.

Although equipped with excellent armour and a powerful gun, the Chieftain was underpowered, with an unreliable power pack, and, despite improved TN37 transmission, the Shir Iran 1 – planned to enter service with three to-be-established armoured divisions – suffered the same problem, with the Armoured Trials and Development Unit having to replace the power pack every 39 miles.[24]

The Shah also purchased Soviet equipment worth $110 million in January 1967, including BTR-50 and BTR-152 APCs, between 100 and 170 122mm calibre D-30 howitzers, 72 BM-21 MLRS and around 200 ZSU-23-4 and ZSU-57-2 self-propelled anti-aircraft guns.[25] However, potentially one of the most important Iranian purchases from the Soviet Union took place only in 1977, when Iran placed an order for 18 9P117 transporter-erector-launchers (TELs) and 36 R-17E Elbrus (ASCC code SS-1c Scud-B) surface-to-surface missiles for an entirely new unit that was in the process of being established at a newly-constructed, underground base north of Khorramabad. The unit and base were about 80 percent complete, but only eight TELs and a few missiles were delivered by the time of the revolution in 1979. Further development of this capability was suspended and the Khorramabad base – and all the weapons stored inside bunkers there – practically abandoned: indeed, the new Islamic government subsequently banned the procurement of ballistic missiles.[26]

The IRIA did possess one advantage over the Iraqis in a substantial, well-balanced and well-trained army air corps (Islamic Republic of Iran Army Aviation, IRIAA). This huge force operated over 1,000 helicopters and was originally planned to become the core of three air cavalry divisions and then five air groups.

On 6 March 1979, the new government in Tehran renounced Iran's role as 'policeman of the Gulf', slashed the military budget, cancelled all major related contracts, refused to accept delivery of most of the equipment ordered in the USA and UK, and began to expel Western instructors and technicians. Failing to recognize the importance of the military as a shield against foreign aggression and a prime COIN asset, the revolutionaries watched as thousands of officers and NCOs were demobilized or arrested during the following months. Never trusting even those units that proved loyal to his regime, Khomeini was anxious to retain only about a third of the total force once it was 'reformed'.

In the summer of 1980, the acting Commander-in-Chief of the military was President Abol Hassan Bani-Sadr, who had supported Khomeini during his exile in France and was a clergyman's son. The armed forces were now led by nine officers who had been former prisoners of the Shah, while a retired Special Forces officer, Colonel Nasrollah Tavakkoli, advised Khomeini. He suggested which officers were more supportive of the new regime, while clerical officers were assigned to all headquarters to act like Soviet commissars. The Islamic Revolution was generally supported by the rank and file and many junior officers, especially technicians. Senior officers were either more ambivalent or hostile, and it was these who bore the brunt of a series of purges, in the course of which between 10,000 and 12,000 military personnel were removed, mostly from the Army, by mid-1980. These included up to 40 percent of the 36,480 officer corps. Contrary to reports about widespread executions, 'only' 77 Army officers were executed, 42 were jailed and 215 were retired, although others fled abroad. The executed included 26 of 180 generals, mostly closely linked with the old regime and including members of the paramilitary or security forces.[27] Some 500 senior officers, including every division and brigade commander, were dismissed, but only 0.05 percent of the Army's medium-level officers suffered and almost none of the junior officers.[28]

Irrespective of statistics, the atmosphere of suspicion caused thousands of junior officers and skilled technicians voluntarily to leave: one estimate suggests up to half of the medium-level officers (majors and colonels) left because suspicious clerics questioned their orders and repeatedly disrupted their command. The purges and enforced retirements meant that divisions, brigades and battalions

After studying US experiences from the Vietnam War, the Iranian Army began developing its own version of 'airborne cavalry', and placed huge orders for helicopters of US origin. The centrepiece of the new service became 202 Bell AH-1J Cobra attack helicopters. (Tom Cooper Collection)

The major medium transport helicopter type of the newly established Imperial Iranian Army Aviation (later Islamic Republic of Iran Army Aviation) became 287 Bell 214A Esfahans. The Iranians originally planned to launch domestic production of further much-improved variants of this type in the 1980s. (Tom Cooper Collection)

The IIAA and IIAF ordered a total of 86 Boeing-Meridionali CH-47C Chinook helicopters in the late 1970s, about 67 of which were eventually delivered (some of them as late as 1981). (Albert Grandolini Collection)

were led by inexperienced officers and operated with limited capability. Some 30 percent of IRIA equipment was non operational, as well as 60 percent of IRIA and IRIAA helicopters, while, despite the acquisition of 10 years' worth of spares during the 1970s, the entire support infrastructure collapsed during the chaos of revolution, and there were already shortages of these, as well as ammunition, communications equipment, transport vehicles and even food.

Khomeini demanded the restoration of discipline but this proved very difficult and slow to implement under prevalent circumstances. Clerical fears of a coup and personnel unrest meant that not only training using live ammunition ceased, but also all sorts of periodic maintenance, while armoured units were largely confined to simulators or classrooms as clerical demands for religious instruction and political indoctrination undermined even basic training. Furthermore, there remained within the IRIA sufficient loyalists to plot coups.

The last major attempt was the 'Nojeh Coup'. This was thwarted (apparently with some help from Soviet intelligence agencies) in July 1980 and involved 280 officers – primarily from the 92nd Arm Div and 55th Airborne Brigade – who were arrested, with many executed.

IRIA formations thus became little more than shells: the Army shrank from 190,000 to 100,000 by mid-1980, as troops quit their barracks with small arms and ammunition to join various militia groups. Yet the IRIA remained the foundation of the new regime's security against a variety of threats, including revolutionary groups who had formerly been Khomeini's allies, such as the People's Struggle (Mojahedin-e Khalq or Mojahedin), the People's Guerrillas (Cherikha-ye Faday-e Khalq or Fadaeeyan) and the Masses Party (Tudeh), which was a pseudo-Communist organization. There were also rebellions by ethnic minorities living near the borders; the Kurdish one being the largest, which was suppressed only in 1988 with the IRIA alone suffering 3,000 casualties, in addition to revolts among the Baluchs in the east and, briefly, the Arabs in the west.[29]

With the merging of the two Imperial Guard Divisions around Tehran into the 21st Inf Div, the IRIA was left with a total of 30 manoeuvre brigades, mostly organic to seven divisions (see Order of Battle), which usually had the equivalent of an extra manoeuvre brigade in division troops, five artillery and three engineer groups. It remained distributed as it had been under the Shah, with most units facing Iraq, but while these were formerly under the I Corps headquarters at Khermanshah, this and the other corps were dissolved during the revolution. From north to south, this had commanded the 64th Inf Div (at Urmia, also written Orumiyeh), 28th Inf Div (Sanandaj), 81st Arm Div (Kermanshah) and 92nd Arm Div (Ahvaz), as well as the 40th (Sarab) and 84th (Khorramabad) Independent Infantry Brigades. Each armoured division had six tank and five mechanized infantry battalions organized into three brigades, but by 1980 they were each able to deploy only one under-strength brigade along the border to Iraq.[30] As a strategic reserve, the Tehran-based II Corps had had the 16th Arm Div (Qazvin), 21st Inf Div and 23rd SF Bde (Nohed), while to the south had been III Corps at Shiraz, with 37th Arm Bde and 55th Air Bde. Watching Afghanistan was the task of the Mashhad-based 77th Inf Div and 30th Infantry Brigade (Gorgan), while the 88th Arm Bde (later expanded into a division) was created at Zahedan as the cadre for a planned fourth corps at Chahbahar. The Navy had two Marine battalions.

There was also a paramilitary force, the Iranian Islamic Gendarmerie

As well as nearly 1,000 helicopters, Iranian Army Aviation operated a miscellany of nearly 100 light and medium-sized transport aircraft, including the Fokker F.27. Like the entire service, they saw intensive deployment during the war with Iraq. (Tom Cooper Collection)

One of the 20 Agusta-Sikorsky AS-61A-4 Sea King helicopters of the Iranian Navy, seen shortly prior to delivery in the 1970s. Although configured for anti-submarine and anti-surface warfare, they saw frequent deployment in relation to operations of Iranian special forces, especially the Special Boat Service. (Albert Grandolini Collection)

The creation of the Iraqi military was strongly influenced by the British, and British-made equipment was dominant even in the late 1960s. This double column of Churchill tanks (with a few Centurions in the background) took part in a military parade in 1954. (Albert Grandolini Collection)

Starting in 1956, the USA began donating armament to the Iraqi military too. Included was a batch of M24 Chafee light tanks, several of which can be seen here, together with half a dozen British-made Ferret armoured cars. US-Iraqi military co-operation was rudely interrupted by the February 1958 Revolution. (Albert Grandolini Collection)

(IIG) formerly the Imperial Gendarmerie about 75,000 strong (half of them conscripts) as of early 1979. Subjected to the Ministry of Interior, the IIG was responsible for rural law enforcement and border security. It was organized into 16 districts, each of which had two to five 'regiments' for a total of some 250 companies. The IIG units were equipped with BTR-60 APCs, light anti-tank weapons such as bazookas and RPG-7s, and 6081mm mortars, and operated an excellent communications system. While its strength dropped to about 40,000 in mid-1980, it still operated a number of posts along the border to Iraq, each with up to 20 men, supported by 'strike' companies and 81mm mortars, all linked by VHF radio: they were to play an important role in the early battles against invaders.[31]

As well as tanks and armoured cars, the majority of the Iraqi Army's artillery for much of the mid-twentieth century was British-made too. This photograph from the mid-1950s shows a battery of the famous 25 pdrs. (Albert Grandolini Collection)

The most powerful main battle tank (MBT) of the Iraqi Army in the late 1950s and much of the 1960s was the British-made Centurion. Replaced by T-55s, most seem to have eventually been donated to Jordan in the late 1960s. (Albert Grandolini Collection)

Starting in 1958, but especially following the June 1967 Arab-Israeli War, Iraq began importing about 800 T-54 and T-55 MBTs from the USSR and Czechoslovakia. This example is shown somewhere on the front line east of Basra, early during the war with Iran. (Albert Grandolini Collection)

The most modern MBT of the Iraqi Army in September 1980 was the T-72, about 155 of which were in service exclusively with the much-dreaded 10th Armoured Brigade. Moscow was so annoyed by Saddam's decision to invade Iran without bothering to inform it, that another shipment of 139 T-72 underway to Iraq was promptly ordered back to the Soviet Union. Soviet-built tanks exported to the Middle East usually arrived with most of their crucial equipment separated from the vehicle: instructions in English applied within the vehicle usually marked where this equipment was to be installed.
(Albert Grandolini Collection)

The primary armoured personnel carrier (APC) in Iraqi mechanized infantry formations in the 1970s and early 1980s was the OT-62 a Czechoslovak-manufactured variant of the BTR-50 395 of which were acquired in the early 1970s. The vehicle used the chassis of the PT-76 reconnaissance tank and could carry up to 20 troops.
(Albert Grandolini Collection)

Khomeini's regime perceived the United States as the prime enemy, and its clerics were virulently opposed to the 'corrupt' West. Iran's anti-US policy led Washington to withdraw some 6,500 advisors and technical experts vital to the running of the armed forces, who took with them most of the computerised records of the Shah's logistical system. The administration of US President Jimmy Carter did seek an accommodation with new government in Tehran, which in August 1979 cancelled military equipment orders worth $8 billion. However, in November of the same year, the American Embassy was occupied by demonstrators, who took hostage most of the staff.[32] Unable to achieve a diplomatic solution, Washington, which had frozen $6 billion worth of Iranian assets (including $900 million of military spares), tried a covert military rescue operation in April 1980, but this turned into a bloody and embarrassing farce which heightened Tehran's fear of what the clergy called 'The Great Satan'. The hostages were eventually freed in January 1981, on the same day a new US president, Ronald Reagan, was inaugurated.

The shortages of both technicians and spare parts especially plagued the Islamic Republic of Iran Air Force (IRIAF), which had 15 combat squadrons in the west, nine along the coast and seven acting as a strategic reserve, with a total nominal strength of 445 combat aircraft. While the Iraqis expected Iranian serviceability rates of 3040 percent for fighters and 50 percent for helicopters, the condition of the air force was actually slightly better, although by August 1980 all the personnel were in urgent need of refresher training. The situation was similar in the case of the IRIA, which had about 500 tanks, of which 300 were operational, but the Iranians could man only a fraction of them because of personnel shortages. Much more damaging were massive purges of top officers, which caused disrupted chains of command in all services, making inexperienced novice commanders heavily dependent on pre-1978 planning in the case of a war, much of which was either obsolete or betrayed to the Iraqis.[33]

Clerical suspicion of the IRIA led the new regime to create its own forces, both to meet internal threats and to counterbalance the Army. In April 1979, the Islamic Army of the Guardians of the Islamic Revolution (Sepah-e Pasdaran-e Enghelab-e Eslami or Pasdaran) – officially reorganized as the Islamic Revolutionary Guards Corps (IRGC) in January 1981 – was founded.[34] The new constitution, ratified in December 1979, stated: "The Army of the Islamic Republic and the Guards Corps of the Revolution will be responsible not only for defending the borders , but also for the ideological mission of holy war in the way of God and fighting to expand the rule of God's law in the world." Paragraph 150 noted the Pasdaran would 'continue its role in guarding the revolution and its offshoots', or, as one writer observed, that the Pasdaran's 'military, religious, and revolutionary mandates are intertwined'.[35]

The Pasdaran had a triumvirate leadership: Mohsen Rezai was the military leader, Mohsen Rafiq-Dust the Pasdaran Minister in the government, with Ali Riza Afshar responsible for the 'staff'. By the summer of 1980, they commanded some 30,000 men organized into 10 provincial areas and deployed in combat or protection units, each of two 10-man teams or squads.[36] They were augmented by the National Mobilisation Organization (Sazman-e Basij-e Milli), more commonly called the Mobilization of the Oppressed (Basij-e Mustazafin, or Basiji), created in November 1979 as a 75,000-strong popular force to defend the revolution. Basiji primarily consisted of young, uneducated and usually rural poor who volunteered for the role.[37] Despite the national framework, both militias remained at

The primary APC of the Iraqi infantry in the early 1980s was the BTR-60. This wheeled vehicle was amphibious and could carry 16 troops. (Albert Grandolini Collection)

The BMP-1 infantry fighting vehicle was still a relatively newcomer in the Iraqi Army, although up to 620 were acquired before September 1980. Equipped with a 73mm gun and 9K11 Malyutka (AT-3 Sagger) anti-tank missile, it became the primary vehicle of the Iraqi mechanized infantry during the war with Iran. (Albert Grandolini Collection)

In order to even out the Iranian advantage in mobile artillery, the Iraqis purchased a total of 85 155mm AUF1 self-propelled howitzers from France, starting in 1983. The system proved reliable and was still in use in 1991, when this example was captured by the US Army. (Albert Grandolini Collection)

local level extremely autonomous, under the control of individual clerics who were often jockeying for power, and enforced their views, accepting or ignoring central control as they wished. The units in Khorasan, for example, ignored mobilization orders from Tehran, as did others if they were signed by an official of whom they did not approve.[38]

The Pasdaran and IRIA leaders co-operated in counter-insurgency operations, especially in Kurdistan, but mutual suspicions remained.

Another attempt at equalizing Iran's advantage in mobile artillery resulted in Iraq adapting various artillery pieces on a surplus chassis of Soviet-made tanks. This former T-34 received what appears to be a 100mm T-12 anti-tank gun with shield. (Albert Grandolini Collection)

During the summer of 1980, the newly established Iraqi Army Aviation Corps received the first batch of 12 Mil Mi-25 helicopter gunships. This heavily armed, armoured and fast type saw intensive service during the war with Iran. (Ali Tobchi Collection)

Between 1977 and 1984, Iraq acquired a total of 35 SA.342M, 56 SA.342K and 20 SA.342H Gazelle helicopters from France, which formed the backbone of light attack units assigned to all three wings of the IrAAC in the early years of the war. (Ali Tobchi Collection)

In many respects, the IRIA had an advantage, for it retained specialists such as tank and artillery crews, few of whom appear to have wished to join the Pasdaran. Some senior IRIA leaders desired closer co-operation bordering on integration, but Defence Minister Mostofa Ali Chamran was more interested in converting the armed forces into supporters of the revolution.

Chapter 2 Notes

1. For the Iraqi Republic Army before 1980, see Al-Marashi & Salama, pp.10728; Pollack, *Arabs*, pp.15682; Murray & Woods, pp.5266.
2. Pollack, *Arabs*, pp.16776; Dupuy, *Elusive Victory*, pp.46769, 53335.
3. Details of military equipment performance and sales based upon DIA DDB-1100-IZ-81, pp.Xxxixxxiii; Christopher Foss, *Jane's Armour and Artillery*, various editions, hereafter Foss; and Jacques de Lestapis, *Military Powers Encyclopedia*, hereafter Lestapis. See also Murray and Woods, Table 5.1. Following the 1972 Friendship and Co-operation Treaty with Moscow,1,600 Russian tanks were delivered. In addition, Iraq retained some of the 135 M-30 122mm howitzers and 60 A-19 122mm guns it had received earlier, the former in mountain divisions. British 25 pdr (87mm) gun-howitzers and 5.5in (139.7mm) howitzers inherited from the British were held in store and would be used in small numbers during the Iran-Iraq War. The Iraqis also retained, and would use, a small number of Soviet SU-100 armoured, self-propelled assault guns.
4. DIA DDB-1100-IZ-81, pp.89,75. Also SIPRI Trade Register 1980.
5. Interviews with IRIA veterans, including former NCOs of the 88th and 92nd Arm Div.
6. The ERC-TH were delivered from 1981. Contrary to many reports, Paris did not supply Iraq with AMX-30 tanks.
7. SIPRI claims 100 EE-11 Urutu wheeled APC were also supplied, but they appear to have arrived later.
8. IDF Journal, Volume III No.2 (spring 1986). Jeff Abramowitz, Jacqueline Hahn, Jerry Cheslow (based on IDF Intelligence Branch briefings), *Iraq: the military build-up*. It is possible that Baghdad augmented 'commercial' acquisitions with Russian MAZ 537G.
9. *Lessons*, p.57; Military Balance 1980. For the Iraqi Army, see also DIA DDB-1100-IZ-81. This estimated (p.6) Iraqi strength in September 1980 at 350,000, with 6,000 AFV and 1,200 guns.
10. Marashi & Salama, p.156; Pollack, *Arabs*, p.182; *Saddam's Generals*, p.129 f/n 137. The order of battle information is based upon UK NA FCO 8/3715 Defence Attache's Annual Report on Iraq, dated 26 June 1980, amended with information from Pesach Malovany.
11. DIA DDB-1100-343-85, p.21.
12. Op cit, pp.3940.
13. Marashi & Salama, pp.12526; Pollack, *Arabs*, p.182; CRRC SH-MISC-D-000-827, p.13.
14. Murray & Woods, pp.5759, 6566.
15. DDB-1100-343-85, pp.2829.

16. Murray & Woods, p.65. The RPG-7 was the prime short-range anti-armour weapon of the Iran-Iraq War and is described by the Russians as a hand-held, anti-tank grenade, but the Western description of Rocket-Propelled Grenade is more accurate. It has an effective range with its 93mm diameter, 2.6kg HEAT warhead, of 200 metres and a maximum range of 920 metres. It is also deadly against infantry, fortifications and even helicopters. See Rottman, *The Rocket Propelled Grenade*, hereafter Rottman.
17. Al-Marashi & Salama, pp.12730.
18. See Perkins' article in the RUSI Journal, but also see Cooper & Bishop, pp.4445; Farrokh, pp.31718; Murray & Woods, pp.7278; Ward, pp.20305; Zabih, *The Iranian military in Revolution and War*, pp.414, hereafter Zabih. Furlong's 1973 article 'Iran A power to be reckoned with'.
19. For the IRIA, see Farrokh, pp.32022; *Lessons*, p.57; Military Balance 1980; Ward pp.19397, 20110; Zabih, pp.314. Website www.Ironsides8m.com/army/ir.htm~army and AllRefer.com, Country Study and Country guide (allrefer.com/country-guide-study), Iran http:allrefer.com/country-guide-study/iran/iran155.html); 'Iran, The Revolutionary Period'; website iiarmy.topcities.com /army/ground/iigf.html.
20. Iran accounted for a third of total US arms sales between 1972 and 1977. Pollack, *The Persian Puzzle*, p.109, hereafter Pollack, *Persians*.
21. Ward, p.196, estimates up to 30 percent of the Imperial Iranian Army were gunners.
22. Details of the Chieftain programmes from UK NA FCO 8 series. Specifically 3124, 3135, 3624, 4164, as well as BT 241/2929 and WO341/204.
23. BT 241/2929. In 2014, the United Kingdom Ministry of Defence was ordered by an international tribunal to pay Iran £390 million for its failure to complete the FV 4030 programme.
24. Production of the Shir Iran began only in March 1979, with the first tanks completed by the end of the year; they were sold to Jordan as the Khalid, in November of the same year.
25. The Iranians also produced the RPG-7 under licence as Sageg. Rottman, p.38.
26. Tom Cooper, 'La Guerre des Villes: Bagdad contre Téhéran', *Air Combat* magazine, No.8/2014.
27. Murray & Woods, p.78 f/n 115.
28. For the impact of the revolution upon the IRIA, see Farrokh pp.11920, 338; Marashi & Salama, p.131; Murray & Woods, pp 8182; Ward, pp. 21125, 22830, 23840, 24445; Zabih, pp.14163.
29. Farrokh, pp.33536; Ward, pp.23134; Zabih, p.237.
30. Website iiarmy.topcities.com/ army/ground/iigf.html.
31. DIA DDB-2680-103-88, pp.2829, and DDB-1100-342-86, p.59.
32. For the hostage crisis, see Farrokh, pp.33941; Pollack, *Persians*, pp.15380; Ward, pp.23637.
33. For the status of Iranian forces, see Buchan, *Days of God*, p.341, hereafter Buchan; Cooper & Bishop, pp.5051; Farrokh, pp.32930, 33536, 33839, 348, 453 f/n 34; Pollack, *Persians*, p.186. CRRC SH-GMD-D-000-842.
34. Farrokh, pp.33435. Another transliteration is Sipah-i Pasdaran-i Inqilab-i Islami. Annie Tracy Samuel, discussion paper 'Perceptions and Narratives of Security', p.1 f/n 1, hereafter Samuel.
35. Samuel, p.2.
36. Op cit, p.4 f/n 13. DIA DDB-1100-342-86, p.46.
37. Samuel, p.2; Ward, pp.22628. CRRC SH-GMD-D-000-842.
38. Murray & Woods, pp.79, 8183.

3
From Border War to Invasion

When the IRIAF was put on the lowest level of alert, on 8 April 1980, the threat to Iran from the west was growing, but the country's leaders were obsessed with the internal struggle. The Iraqis were very aware the IRIA was a giant with feet of clay. The GMID's 'Report Assessing Political, Military and Economic Conditions in Iran' concluded the Army was poorly led and had no more than 60 percent of its established strength, discipline was weak, morale was low, there was little training and the general deterioration was likely to continue.[1] Led by Brigadier General Abdul Jawad Dhannoun, the GMID had obtained strength returns for the 55th Artillery Group and noted a shortage of privates in a technically based organization. For example, the 394th Artillery Btn had only 58 specialists, although a total of 19 officers and 72 NCOs. This pattern was repeated to a greater or lesser extent throughout the IRIA after all the above-mentioned purges.[2] Furthermore, the GMID noted that the Kurds had inflicted heavy losses on the 28th and 64th Inf Div and 16th Arm Div. It rated the 92nd Arm Div as the best Iranian unit, although badly under strength and running no training at all. The same report concluded that "Iran has no power to launch wide offensive operations against Iraq, or to defend itself on a large scale".[3]

The GMID was a slender reed to lean on for intelligence on Iran. Founded in 1932, it was responsible directly to the president and was responsible for tactical and strategic reconnaissance, as well as monitoring the armed forces' loyalty. In September 1980, its Iran desk had just three officers, of whom only one had studied Farsi. Indeed, there were only three Farsi-speaking officers in the entire Iraqi Army.[4] The GMID had few agents in Iran, and their number further decreased once Khomeini came to power. It lacked accurate maps of the country and was in no condition to decipher enemy communications.[5]

To the US intelligence agencies, the Iraqi 'invasion' of Iran seemed more an increase in intensity of border operations, for tensions between the two countries grew soon after the Shah was deposed.[6] From April 1979, shells and mortar bombs were fired across the border, sparking a series of tit-for-tat raids and bombardments, sometimes involving air strikes which cost both sides aircraft.[7] Although formal preparations for an invasion of Iran did not begin until July, when units were filled out and put in supply requests, there was increased activity in Iraqi maintenance facilities and ammunition dumps from March as training was intensified. By the time Iraqi mobilization began on 4 September, there were clashes and artillery duels along the frontier almost on a daily basis. Some Iranian cities near the border, including Qasr-e Shirin and Mehran, were shelled, while both sides increasingly deployed fixed and rotary-wing aircraft. The superpowers observed this with their satellites but remained unsure what was happening; the Americans thought the preparations were for a major exercise (Nassour 4) in the training grounds near the Jordanian border, until it became clear during the summer that the flow of Iraqi traffic was eastward. Moscow had experts with the Iraqi Army but was also in the dark, despite increasing demands for military equipment from Baghdad.

The scale of fighting slowly increased when the Iraqis began flying air strikes into Iranian Kurdistan, and during the summer there were frequent clashes between border patrols. The Iranians marked the frontier with a line of IIG posts: 29 on the sector south of the Hawizah Marshes (Hawr al Hawizah), underpinned with strongpoints some 3km to the east, sometimes augmented by elements of the IRIA. Each post south of the marshes was reinforced by two dug-in tanks acting as pill-boxes and manned by the 92nd Arm Div's 151st Fortress Btn. The IIG strongpoints were undermanned and ill-equipped; the position covering Shalamcheh had a mechanized infantry unit but was short of food, fuel, ammunition and radios, leaving the men demoralized.[8] In the face of an increasing number of cross-border raids aimed at 'recovering' disputed border territory, the outgunned and outnumbered Iranians often gave way.

COUNTDOWN TO INVASION

On 4 September 1980, as Iraqi mobilization began, Baghdad accused Tehran of shelling the vicinity of two villages, Zain al-Qaws and Saif Saad, which Iraq was supposed to receive under the Algiers Treaty. The Iraqis now demanded they be handed over, and when this was ignored they seized them on 7 September. The absence of Iranian efforts to recover them encouraged Saddam to nibble away at the frontier. By 10 September, Iraqi troops had taken six border posts and Saddam claimed to have 'recovered' almost all the 240km^2 of territory, including 130km^2 in northern Khuzestan on the border with Maysan Province, which he claimed as owed to his country. The same day, the Iraqis also took a forward communications intelligence (COMINT) base, prompting local Iranian commanders to call the IRIAF to bomb and destroy this facility.

Iran's political leaders remained focused on the internecine conflict and the frontier troubles were, in theatrical terms, 'noises off stage'.[9] US Intelligence noted the Iranians in general –with exception of the IRIA and IRIAF – seemed unwilling, or unable, to grasp the seriousness of the threat. Accompanied by Army leaders, Bani-Sadr toured the Qassr-e-Shirin area on 15 August to discuss the frontier conflict with forward commanders. Together with his entourage, he had a lucky escape when their helicopter suffered an electrical failure and crash-landed. On 9 September, Iran's acting Chief-of-Staff, General Valiollah Fallahi (deputy chairman of the Joint Chiefs of Staff), with Ground Forces commander General Qasem Ali Zahirnejhad and IRIAF commander Colonel Javad Fakuri, visited Kermanshah Province and discussed the situation with the commander of the 81st Division.[10] This formation, together with elements of the 82nd and 92nd Arm Div, 28th Inf Div and 84th Inf Bde, was responsible for defence of the border to Iraq. But it was able to deploy only seriously understrength brigades, most of which were battalion-sized task forces. In Khuzestan, these were supported by the 22nd and 55th Artillery Groups.

A Chieftain of the Imperial Guards (later 21st Infantry) Division drives up to support police guarding an official building in Tehran, during the unrest that led to the Shah's overthrow. (Albert Grandolini Collection)

From early September, Tehran made half-hearted attempts to strengthen the border, deploying elements of the 16th IRIA Arm Div, 37th Arm Bde (as Task Force 37), augmented by 13 detachments of the 23rd SF Bde and a part of 55th Air Bde. A battalion-sized task force based on some of these units deployed in the Sardasht area, while individual companies went to Sanandaj and Dezful. Meanwhile, the majority of troops remained either deployed on counter-insurgency operations or restricted to barracks, watched closely by their spiritual advisors.[11]

On 13 September, Khuzestan's Governor, Seyed Mohamad Gharazi, closed the border, and the following afternoon, Bani-Sadr, Premier Mohamad Ali-Rajaie, Fallahi, Zahirnejhad and Javad Fakuri made another tour of inspection near Ilam (capital of Ilam Province) in helicopters, escorted by two Cobras, but their pilots had to make evasive manoeuvres to avoid Iraqi aircraft.[12] Tehran promptly announced that it would no longer abide by the Algiers Treaty, but a

The crew of this Guards Division's Chieftain dispatched to suppress protests clearly changed sides and at some stage fraternized with civilians resulting in their vehicle being decorated with a large photograph of Ayatollah Khomeini. (Albert Grandolini Collection)

day later deployed a large IRIA contingent not to the Iraq border but to Kordistan, which demonstrated Tehran's continued pre-occupation with its internal enemies. It was only after the Iraqi invasion that Bani-Sadr ordered a ceasefire in Kordistan so he could concentrate meagre Army resources in the west.[13]

Just after midnight on 16 September, Saddam presented his plans to both the RCC and the National Command, and revealed he now wanted total control of the Shatt, a decision apparently made a few nights before.[14] The alleged failure of Tehran to implement the Algiers Treaty was Saddam's justification for military action to control the waterway: "We have to stick Iran's head in the mud and force them to say yes so we can get done quickly with this matter." Saddam was asked to clarify Iraq's position with regard to Khuzestan, unofficially called Arabistan because of its substantial Arab population, which had never been part of Iraq. Saddam replied that he would strike into the region only if Tehran contested his claim to the Shatt, and he dismissed questions about the implications for Soviet support, especially regarding the supply of artillery ammunition, if the situation escalated.[15] Contrary to some contemporary claims, it is virtually certain that it was not until November 1980 that he began planning to establish Arabistan as an 'autonomous region closely linked with Iraq'.[16]

On 17 September, Saddam formally abrogated the Algiers Treaty and demanded that Tehran cede control of the Shatt, adding: "We in no way intend to launch war against Iran." While denying any territorial ambitions to Iranian territory, he did demand adjustments to the land frontier and, to strengthen his pan-Arab credentials, the transfer of Abu Musa and the Tunb Islands to the UAE, but he remained silent about Kurdish or Khuzestan Arab autonomy. Bani-Sadr promptly ordered all available IRIA units westwards and summoned the National Security Council to discuss the situation, and after 12 hours it agreed upon a stiff response to the Iraqi attacks. The same day, the Iranian Joint Staff issued its first communiqué rejecting Saddam's demands, although it admitted a full-scale invasion was possible but claimed that Iraq, with US support, had imposed a war upon Iran since the beginning of September. Bani-Sadr also claimed that the Iraqis planned a counter-revolution led by émigré former Iranian Premier Shapour Bakhtiar.

Only a day later, Iraqi forces began attacking Iranian frontier posts in Khuzestan, with the 4th Inf Div advancing on Bostan and 7th Inf Div on Fakkeh.[17] The following day, Iranian naval units in Abadan and Khorramshahr were alerted and naval reservists mobilized.[18] Nevertheless, the 92nd IRIA Arm Div, the backbone of Khuzestan's defence, had been disrupted by the loss of personnel arrested in July, lack of training and lapsed maintenance, so it took several days to deploy company-sized units.[19]

Quite early during the revolution, the Iranian clergy began establishing its own security force. Colloquially known as Pasdaran, these frequently paraded the streets of Tehran sometimes armed with G-3 rifles, as seen here. Before long, they were to become involved in combat operations against various insurgents inside Iran, and then the invading Iraqis. (Albert Grandolini Collection)

Meanwhile, Iraqi forces began deploying eastward, into the area of responsibility of II Corps. The 6th Arm Div was the first to leave its barracks, followed by the 10th Arm Div on 20 September. Within III Corps' area of responsibility, the 1st Mech Div arrived on 5 September, followed by 5th Mech Div about a week later. The 9th Arm Div began deploying along the frontier on 20 September and was followed, two days later, by 3rd Arm Div.[20] I Corps' activity is uncertain, but it probably began deploying elements of its divisions eastwards from early September.

By comparison, the Iranians never managed to build up coherent defences for their frontier, either because the

Often consisting of various local units, the Iranian Gendarmerie was responsible for law and order in rural areas and border defence. The latter was usually controlled from Dezh (fortress) border posts manned by squadrons of up to 20 troops equipped with light infantry weapons, but also bazookas, RPG-7s and some 60mm and 81mm mortars. Iranian Gendarmes suffered heavy losses early during the war with Iraq. (Albert Grandolini Collection)

information was not taken seriously or because internal rivalry prevented Bani-Sadr acting quickly. Only on 20 September did he order the mobilization of the country's almost non-existent reserves, whose organization had collapsed during the revolution.[21] However, Iran did begin evacuating civilians from the frontier region as fighting intensified, the Iraqis seizing more border posts as, from 18 September, the II (al-Yarmouk Force) and III (al-Qadissya Force) Iraqi Corps secured their assembly points (in US terminology, 'line-of-departure') from enemy artillery, using 17th SF Bde from the 6th Arm Div and 1st Mech Div to establish positions.[22]

On 21 September, as Tehran ordered conscript soldiers discharged the previous year to return to the colours, the IrAF received orders to strike at eight IRIAF air bases and two major bases of the IRIA within the range of available aircraft. A day later, 192 Iraqi bombers and fighter-bombers pressed home their attack, opening the war.

OPENING BLOWS

The opening strike of the Iraqi Air Force was not, as so often claimed, intended to emulate the crushing success of the Israeli air force offensive at the beginning of the June 1967 Arab-Israeli War. Instead, it was primarily intended to crater runways on Iranian air bases and thus render them inoperational for the first 48 hours of the Iraqi offensive, and increase already widespread chaos in Iranian armed forces.[23] Correspondingly, only three IRIAF aircraft were destroyed on the ground.[24]

Even so, these raids cost the Iraqis not only one Tu-16 (ASCC code Badger) bomber and three fighter-bombers, but had no significant effect upon the IRIAF: acting according to long-established plans in case of a war with Iraq (further updated on 18 August), the Iranians returned the favour by launching about 70 combat sorties – including several raids on Iraqi air bases – within only two hours of the first Iraqi attack. Furthermore, on the following morning, the IRIAF launched Operation Kaman-99, deploying 129 F-4 Phantoms and F-5 Tigers in a major air strike on 15 Iraqi air bases, oil installations and other facilities. While losing nine aircraft in the process (at least four of these to mechanical malfunctions), the Iranians claimed destruction of 20 IrAF aircraft on the ground (the Iraqis confirmed only two of these).[25]

This was the main effect of the opening Iraqi air strike, and for the first 48 hours of the war, large Iraqi mechanized forces were able to roam the flat terrain of south-western Khuzestan largely unmolested by the IRIAF. Overall, the Iraqis committed all or parts of eight divisions, totalling about 98,000 men, 1,500 tanks and 520 artillery pieces.[26] By November 1980, this force was reinforced through three additional divisions (35,000 men) of the Army and 40,000 troops of the Popular Army (the latter primarily deployed to guard lines of communication).[27]

Because Iraqi Corps and Division commanders never received clear instructions from Saddam, the invasion was made on six uncoordinated axes, whose general objective was the line connecting Musian-Susangerd-Ahvaz-Khorramshahr to create a bridgehead which they would fortify and hold. The planners ignored the highways which ran parallel with the frontier just beyond this line, which would be the backbone for their Operational Level supply system and springboards for further offensives, and also failed to seize the mountain passes, through which men and materiel flowed to Khuzestan from Tehran.[28]

The Iraqi operation was a land grab rather than a properly run military invasion. It eventually did penetrate as deep as 65km into Iran, but in most places it remained rather shallow, with an average depth of 2040km. Even so, the Iraqis eventually found themselves in possession of about 10,686km² of Iranian territory.[29] Although the Iraqis possessed the advantage in COMINT during the early months of the war, because Iranians communicated *en clair*, they failed to exploit this factor.[30] One reason for the shallow advance was a logistics system based upon that of the Soviet Army: the so-called 'supply push' philosophy, in which materiel was automatically sent forward to meet anticipated demand, rather than the 'demand pull' system, which responds to the units' actual requirements. This emptied Iraqi Army supply depots within a week, although much materiel was simply held by the forward units.[31]

HELICOPTER SUPPORT

Despite the many shortcomings of their military, sheer numerical superiority usually resulted in the Iraqis overpowering their opponents. True enough, the Iraqi planning and execution of military operations improved considerably through the 1970s –also at a tactical level – and the Iranians still suffered terribly due to revolutionary chaos. However, many Iraqi brigade, division and even corps COs proved inadequate and outright incompetent at operational and strategic levels. Worse still, Saddam insisted on painstakingly monitoring all battlefield activity and repeatedly meddled in command decisions with entirely useless suggestions and orders. This resulted in his subordinates finding themselves forced to ignore the realities of the battlefield and produce wildly exaggerated estimates of enemy strength to explain their sluggish advance.[32] Already by November 1980, it was noticeable that Iraqi troops would break under pressure; 'the Iraqi spirit I always feared', as Saddam put it. The head of the presidential secretariat, Tariq Hamed al-Abdullah, commented: 'That is why our mobile defence fails … we always (abandon) land.'[33]

Helicopters would play a major role supporting the armies during the next eight years. The IRIAA operated 740 helicopter gunships and other combat-support types in 29 squadrons, dwarfing the 260 of the Iraqi Army Air Corps' (IrAAC) eight squadrons. Types in service ranged from the light (under 5 tonnes take-off weight) observation models such as the Augusta Bell 206A Jet Ranger in Iran and Aerospatiale SA 316C Alouette and SA 342 Gazelle in Iraq; to medium weight (512 tonnes take-off weight) utility transport aircraft such as the Agusta Bell 205A Iroquois and Bell 214 A/C Esfahan in Iran, and Mil Mi-8 (ASCC-code Hip C) in Iraq; and heavy (12 tonnes and above) transports such as the Meridionali-Vertol CH-47C Chinook in Iran and Aerospatiale SA 321 Super Frelon in Iraq.

Both sides began deploying large numbers of armed helicopters (gunships), though tactics employed were entirely different. Around 200 purpose-built, armoured Bell AH-1J Cobras of the IRIAA usually made low-level, terrain-following approaches to the battlefield, detected targets with the aid of M65 electro-optical sights, then climbed to launch BGM-71 TOW wire-guided anti-tank missiles (ATGMs) with a maximum range of 4.2km. Additionally, they had a 20mm three-barrel gun for attacks on 'soft' targets, light armour and 68mm calibre unguided rockets.[34] The combat radius of the AH-1J was about 290km.

The Iraqis had nothing comparable to the AH-1J. The most similar in terms of anti-tank capability and armour were about 20 of the much bigger and heavier Mil Mi-25 Hind helicopter gunships. However, their 9K17 Skorpion (Scorpion) (ASCC code AT-2B Swatter B) ATGMs were obsolete and these heavy helicopters were

Ironically, the first combat mission of the Iranian Army Aviation was an operation against Kurdish insurgents in north-western Iran in late 1979. Lieutenant Ahmed Keshavari and his colleagues are shown with one of the AH-1Js during pre-revolutionary training in Esfahan. (via N.R.)

Iranian Kurds proved to be good marksmen and managed to shoot down a number of IRIAA helicopters. Interestingly, the Iranian military recovered every piece of wreckage it could get its hands on, and most of the wrecked Cobras and Esfahans visible on this photograph were subsequently repaired and returned to service, or recycled for spares. (via N.R.)

unable to hover, so their crews flew them as fighter-bombers. About 40 Gazelles, originally purchased by the IrAF but in service with the IrAAC by August 1980, were fast and nimble. Some were equipped with the SFIM APX-Bézu 334 or APX-397 gyro-stabilized sights and could be armed with up to four French-made HOT ATGMs with a maximum range of 4.3km. When deploying such weapons, they operated in similar fashion to IRIAA Cobras. However, they lacked armour and their 'glasshouse' type cockpit proved very vulnerable, even to small arms fire. Nevertheless, for operations in 'low threat' areas, Gazelles were regularly armed with 20mm cannons installed inside the cabin and firing through the left door. Both sides' daylight operations benefitted from television-based sighting systems and laser rangefinders, but night-time operations were severely restricted by the absence of thermal imagers and the shortage of image-intensifiers, especially night vision goggles.[35]

EARLY BATTLES

On 28 September, after concluding he had achieved most of his territorial objectives, Saddam said he would accept a ceasefire, provided Tehran accepted Iraq's total rights over the Shatt and 'usurped Iraqi territories', and withdrew from the disputed islands in the Gulf. Actually, by this time the Iraqi military began to feel the power of the IRIAF, which was now not only unleashing regular strikes against the Iraqi oil industry, but also launched an all-out effort against enemy mechanized forces in Khuzestan. That day, the UN Security Council called for an end to hostilities and mediation on the dispute, while several organizations also offered to mediate. On 4 October, the Iraqi Army was ordered to destroy the captured border posts and tear up the frontier markers, and the following day Saddam announced a unilateral ceasefire, designed both to give the enemy time to seek terms and his own forces to rest and regroup.[36] However, this was little else but a propaganda effort: the fact was that by this time a few scattered task forces of the IRIA and three wings of the IRIAF were so effectively fighting the Iraqis in Khuzestan Province that the invasion was *de facto* brought to a standstill.

Unsurprisingly considering this, Tehran rejected both the ceasefire and all offers of mediation, then set its own price for peace as an immediate and rapid Iraqi withdrawal from the occupied territories, Saddam's resignation, $130 billion reparations (with Basra placed in Iranian hands as security) and autonomy for Iraqi Kurds. Nationalist emotion in response to the invasion boosted the Iranian regime: not only that, even Khuzestan's Sunni Arabs remained loyal to Iran (indeed one of them, Ali Shamkhani would later become Iranian Defence Minister), and their armed forces were soon bitterly fighting the Iraqis at every opportunity. If Tehran was serious with these demands, then it – just like Saddam before – badly over-estimated its position. The diplomatic impasse continued for a month, during which it has been suggested that the clerics rejected Saddam's terms because the war provided a useful instrument with which to beat their 'unpatriotic' secular enemies.[37]

When Saddam finally recognized there would be no immediate negotiated solution, he ordered his forces to renew their advance in November 1980. Progress was again slow and ended with the onset of the rainy season, which continued until early March and converted much of the battlefield into a swamp.[38] Within six weeks of the invasion, Saddam appears to have become concerned that he had the tiger by the tail. Not only had the IRIAF knocked out most of the Iraqi oil industry, forcing the country to stop exports and start importing fuel, but the Army also proved unable to maintain its momentum. Nevertheless, on 30 October he assured his cronies the enemy was on the verge of defeat, although warning that it might take another six to 12 months. In typical fashion of a contradictive dictator, during a speech to the National Assembly on 4 November 1980, he admitted he now knew 'it would have been better if we did not go to war. But we had no other choice'.[39]

The Americans noted the advance appeared to meet little resistance at first, for the Iranians were stunned by Saddam's actions and only 25,000 members of the IRIA and IIG were deployed along the frontier.[40] Initially, resistance was sporadic and uncoordinated, with Gendarmerie, border police, volunteers and Pasdaran setting up road blocks or ambushes, then retreating or changing position without any apparent order or purpose. This led to the loss of much equipment, often after only token resistance.[41] There were a few exceptions to this rule, one of these being Task Force 37. Deployed to the frontline as the first Iranian armoured formation, it found itself equipped with only six M47Ms (two were unserviceable) and five M60A1s (one unserviceable) on the afternoon of 22 September. Nevertheless, it knocked out 18 Iraqi tanks during the fighting near the Fakkeh border

The crew of an Iraqi T-55 probably from the 5th Mechanized Division seen west of Khorramshahr, waiting for orders to invade Iran, in September 1980. Contrary to their expectations, that undertaking proved a major challenge for the Iraqi armoured juggernaut. (Albert Grandolini Collection)

post that day. By the next morning, the task force was down to three runners (two M60A1s and one M47M), but it not only knocked out another 15 Iraqi tanks but also successfully evacuated all eight tanks damaged the previous day. The task force continued in this fashion for several weeks thanks to plentiful provision of close-air-support (CAS) by the IRIAF and IRIAA, skilful manoeuvring, repeated counterattacks into Iraqi flanks and sporadic reinforcements in the form of small groups of Chieftains from the 92nd Arm Div, together with hundreds of CAS sorties by Dezful-based F-5Es. Ultimately, it stopped the Iraqi advance upon Dezful in October.

Overall, the Iraqis claimed to have taken 10,000 prisoners of war (POWs), of which about 15 percent were junior officers and NCOs, some being paramilitary troops, although many of these were shot out of hand.[42] Actually, Iranian losses in manpower and materiel were minimal because – despite many claims of the contrary – they had very few military units deployed along the border to Iraq.

Curiously, US intelligence organizations such as the Defense Intelligence Agency largely ignored the presence of Iranian paramilitary forces, probably because they were no match for the Iraqis in open country where the Iranians, before the revolution, had planned to rely upon IRIA armoured units. Immediately after the invasion, the Iranian armoured brigades were reinforced by elements of 21st and 77th IRIA Inf Divs and the 84th Inf Bde. Most of the divisional artilleries were also deployed, some before the invasion, and their skilful use began to be another important factor encouraging Iraqi caution. As the Iranians recovered, they began making more effective use of their US-supplied heavy weapons, especially gunships and artillery, augmented by the Russian MLRSs, despite frequent problems with ammunition supply. Ironically, despite the success of the IRIA, Iran's political leaders appear to have preferred to encourage the Pasdaran and Basij volunteers to provide the backbone of the defence, and significant elements of the IRIA, including the 88th Arm Div, and 28th and 64th Inf Divs, remained in barracks during most of October and even later.[43]

Chapter 3 Notes
1. CRRC SH-GMD-D-000-842. See also Hiro, p.49.
2. *Lessons*, p.41.
3. CRRC SH-GMD-D-000-842.
4. Even the following year, the Iranian section had only six.
5. For the GMID, see Marashi & Salama, pp.14647; *Saddam's Generals*, pp.20, 89.
6. For the border fighting, see Cooper & Bishop, pp.6368; Farrokh, pp.34445; Malovany, pp.18122, 12425; Murray & Woods, pp.9192;CRRC SH –SHTP-A-000-835 and US Army Intelligence and Security Command history, pp.4.2, 4.5, hereafter US AISC.
7. See Cooper & Bishop, pp.6368.
8. Parviz Mosalla Nejad (ed.), *Shalamcheh*, pp.910, hereafter Nejad.
9. See Murray & Woods, p.93.
10. US AISC, pp.4.2, 4.5.
11. Op cit, p.4.9.
12. Cooper & Bishop, p.67; Nejad, p.10.
13. Even then, the IRGC ignored his orders, see Farrokh, p.349; Ward p.247.
14. CRRC SH –SHTP-A-000-835. This is the CRRC heading, but Murray & Woods, p.49 f/n 137, state the document is entitled 'Meeting Between Saddam Hussein, the National Command and the Revolutionary Command Council Discussing the Iran-Iraq War, 16 September 1980'.
15. For the Iraqi decision to go to war, see Murray & Woods, pp.4850, 9398.
16. Murray & Woods, p.114.
17 Farrokh, pp.34445.
18. Farrokh, pp.34950;Ward, p.244; US AISC, p.4.5.
19. Ward, p.251.
20. US AISC, p.4.6.
21. Op cit, p.244.
22 . Cooper & Bishop, pp.7781; *Project 1946*, pp.4748.
23. Sadik, interview, March 2005.
24. Cooper et al article, *La Guerre Iran-Irak*, Volume 1, hereafter Guerre Vol.1.
25. Cooper & Bishop, pp.7275; *La Guerre*, pp.4244; Malovany, pp.12529; Murray & Woods, pp.10008; US AISC, p.4.5.
26. These figures are based upon the order-of-battle and ASIC data. Sources quoting larger figures assume the whole Iraqi Army was deployed in the invasion.
27. J. Wagner, 'Iraq', in Gabriel, *Fighting Armies*, p.68.
28. See comments by Murray & Woods, pp.108 and f/n 80, 114, 124, 131.
29. Griffin, *The Iraqi Way of War*, p.18, hereafter Griffin.
30. Op cit, pp.2021.
31. *Saddam's Generals*, pp.12830.
32. Murray & Woods, pp.116 f/n 97, 118.
33. Op cit, p.113.
34. SIPRI data suggests Iran received 23,800 TOW missiles before the

Revolution. Saddam was so impressed by the obvious superiority of these weapons over the Russian missiles used by his helicopters that in January 1981 he asked his staff to seek TOW missiles and launchers from the Saudis and Jordanians. Murray & Woods, p.154.

35. For the air war, see Cooper & Bishop and the same authors' article 'Fire in the Hills'. This passage benefits from information provided by both authors.
36. Buchan, p.339; Pollack, *Arabs*, p.193.
37. Murray & Woods, p.117.
38. O'Ballance, p.41.
39. Murray & Woods, pp.116, 125.
40. Farrokh, p.350.
41. Ward, p.251. US AISC, pp.4.9, 4.11, 4.454.47.
42. Zabih, p.134 f/n 30.
43. US AISC, p.4.9.

4
The Invasion of Khuzestan

Khuzestan is Iran's prime source of hydro-carbons, with the Abadan refinery providing much of the country's refining capacity at 630,000 barrels a day. With these resources Saddam could rival Saudi Arabia, and he hoped for local support because a third of the province's 3.1 million population are Arabs. In April 1979, they had staged demonstrations in Khorramshahr for greater autonomy, but the Pasdaran and marines soon crushed this movement, losing a dozen Pasder and killing 100 Arabs.[1]

Saddam was indifferent to their fate; his prime objective was to control the Shatt. Lieutenant General Isma'ail Tayeh Ni'ami's III Corps was to take the northern bank by mid-September, then capture Abadan, both to deprive Iran of its largest refinery and to threaten the oil fields. The campaign saw a noticeable lack of support from Khuzestan's Arabs because of the brutal repression of the Iraqi Army, notably 9th Arm Div's commander, Brigadier General Talia Khalil Al-Duri, who was praised by Saddam for executing 56 members of one tribe.[2] As a result, resistance within the province would be the fiercest and most effective encountered by the Iraqis.

Saddam's strategy also ignored the terrain. Khuzestan is bounded in the north-east by the Zagros Mountains (Kuhha-ye Zagros), which are more than 3,000 metres high and run north-west to south-east across the north-eastern third of the province. The north-western approaches to Khuzestan are through the neighbouring province of Ilam, with a main road running parallel with the international border from Mehran through Dehloran and Musian (also Daskt Mishan), where one fork leads eastward to Dezful down to Fakkeh, all in Ilam Province, with the latter being the gateway to Khuzestan. From there, one road leads north-eastwards to link with the Musian-Dezful road, with a side road from Chananeh (or Cheananeh) to Shush (also called Susa), which lies on the River Karkheh (Rudklianeh-ye Karkheh or Kharkhe Rud).

Between the frontier and the Karkheh is a region of sand dunes rising some 500800 metres above the desert and running roughly east to west. This divided operations from the very beginning of the Iran-Iraq War, and those north of the region will be dealt with in a later volume on the Central and Northern Fronts, while the fighting to the south is described below.

The Karkheh and the Karun (Rud-e Karun) are the major rivers

A platoon of T-62Ms probably from the 3rd Armoured Division advancing line abreast through the desert of western Khuzestan on the first day of the Iraqi invasion, 22 September 1980. Most of the Soviet-made vehicles showed a tendency to overheat in the hot environment because they were designed for operations in entirely different climatic conditions. (Tom Cooper Collection)

A company of Iraqi T-55s lined up for inspection before moving out. (Albert Grandolini Collection)

The crew of an Iraqi Army OT-62 APC seen going into laager at the end of the day, near several T-55s. The soldier to the right is already bringing a can of fresh water for a brew-up. (Albert Grandolini Collection)

The 92nd Armoured Division of the IRIAA included the 151st Fortress Battalion, which operated a number of static M4 Shermans, armed with 105mm howitzers, positioned as pillboxes along the border. All such posts including the one defended by this vehicle were quickly overrun by the Iraqis, sometimes without a shot being fired. (Albert Grandolini Collection)

A pair of Iraqi T-55s probably from the 5th Mechanized Division assemble outside Khorramshahr while their commander examinies terrain ahead. This division lost five such tanks on 3 October 1980 alone. (Albert Grandolini Collection)

Members of the Iranian Gendarmerie posing with their small arms and MG1 machine guns, sometime in mid-September 1980. Most likely, the frontier post in question was overrun by the Iraqis only few days later. (Albert Grandolini Collection)

An Iranian volunteer soldier poses with a US-made M47 Dragon. This small and relatively light anti-tank system fired a missile with a diameter of only 140mm and had a maximum range of 1,500 metres. While its relatively short range made it quite unpopular among US troops, Iranians made extensive use of the Dragon, especially early in the war. Indeed, the effectiveness of the system was such that it prompted the Iraqis to start shopping for it too. (Albert Grandolini Collection)

of Khuzestan. From the mountains, the Karkheh winds southwards through sandy desert, passing Dezful to the west, leaving a marshy trail like a snail. East of Bostan, the waters feed numerous fields criss-crossed with irrigation ditches, then the river passes north of Susangerd (called Khafajiyah by the Arabs). The river is also fed from the west by tributaries from the Hawizah (or Howeizah) Marshes, of which the most important is the River Karkheh Kur in the south, which runs roughly parallel south of the Karkheh before turning sharply north to join it at Hamidiyeh. At Hamidiyeh, the Karkheh also makes a 90° turn north-east to enter the Karun some 35km north of Ahvaz, an oil management and administrative centre, which also controls the main road and rail links to the south. The terrain in the western approaches from Al Amarah to Ahvaz make mechanized movement difficult and confine most traffic to the highway, which skirts the northern edge of the Hawizah Marshes and the northern bank of the Karkheh, which it crosses at Bostan and then runs along the southern bank of the river through Susangerd to Ahvaz.

The Karun, which runs through Ahvaz, is the principal river in south-west Khuzestan and Iran's only navigable inland waterway. South of Ahvaz, it meanders south-south-west, usually through irrigated fields, to empty into the Shatt just south of Khorramshahr (called Muhammarah by the Arabs). Between the river and the Hawizah Marshes is desert, which can become marshy during the winter rains, but in summer, according to British Army maps of 1943, is firm, allowing 1.5-tonne trucks to drive at speeds 'up to 40 mph' (74 km/h). There are some ancient stream beds across this region, where most transport is by minor roads, many of them on embankments, with a junction south-west of Susangerd at Hoveyzeh (also known as Huzgan). On either side of the river are two major, metalled (hard top) highways which lead from Ahvaz in the west to Khorramshahr and to the east to Abadan.

Khorramshahr is a key communications hub, with a railway running alongside the Ahvaz highway and another highway running westwards along the northern bank of the Shatt through the border town of Shalamcheh (in Arabic, Shalmaja) to Basra. This highway ran past numerous palm plantations, which could not be penetrated by armoured vehicles and which could provide cover for infantry movement. Abadan is 8km from Khorramshahr and lies between the Shatt and the salt flats of the Musa Marshes (Khowr-e Musa), which are boggy in the winter but dry out in the summer and can often support the weight of a tank. There are numerous oil and gas fields in these marshes, with highways running eastward to the ports of Bandar-e Emam Khomeini (formerly Bandar-e Shahpur, and for

An Iranian M60 providing cover for infantry during one of many local counter-attacks, launched to keep the invaders off-balance. (Albert Grandolini Collection)

convenience written as Bandar-e Khomeini) and Bandar-e Mashur (also Bande-e Mushahr or Bandar-e Mahshahr).

Ni'ami had retired from the Army in 1978 to become ambassador to Venezuela, then rejoined the colours in 1980 as Deputy Chief of the General Staff, but was given III Corps because he had helped to create it and was familiar both with its mission and leaders.[3] Because the plan assumed there would be no significant opposition from the weakened Iranian Army, Ni'ami allowed the offensive axes to diverge, but with only 20 battalions he faced a chronic shortage of infantry, which would make it difficult to consolidate his gains.

The northern prong consisted of part of the 10th Arm Div and 1st Mech Div, which advanced upon Dezful, north of the dune region (the former reinforced by 10th Arm Bde on 26 September), while to the south, 9th Arm Div drove towards Ahvaz.[4] These moves were intended to prevent reinforcements coming south to Ahvaz and allow 9th Arm Div to link up with the 5th Mech Div, which spearheaded the southern axis. The latter had the most important strategic role in the campaign, to seize Khorramshahr and Abadan, then secure the northern bank of the Shatt al-Arab. Ni'ami had to control two diverging thrusts and, as insurance, he retained 3rd Arm Div in second echelon, but would use its 6th Arm Bde and 8th Mech Bde to isolate Khorramshahr from the north, storm across the River Karun and advance to Abadan.

LEARNING BY EXPERIENCE

Holding the 200km Khuzestan frontier were the IIG, assorted militia and the IRIA's half-strength 92nd Arm Div, augmented by an armoured battalion of 88th Arm Div and an infantry battalion each of 21st and 77th Inf Divs. The 92nd Div was deployed (north to south) with 2nd Bde west of Dezful, 3rd Bde west of Ahvaz and 1st Bde between Ahvaz and Khorramshahr. Iraqi raids left the border forces nervous and near panic when they heard the growing roar of armoured vehicles approaching along the main roads on the morning of 22 September. Some border guards fled, often with civilians from border villages, while others made a brief, heroic but ultimately futile stand against the invaders' heavy weapons and superior numbers.

Yet the Iraqis advanced with painful slowness, beginning each day with a bombardment, often onto empty ground. The subsequent cautious advance was led by tanks whose turrets were swinging backwards and forwards like sniffing dogs, constantly alert to resistance. When they reached their daily objective, the Iraqis would 'circle the wagons', vehicles and troops occupying defensive positions hastily built by engineers to form the following day's jump-off point. Artillery was the weapon of choice to overcome resistance, and while armour might be assembled to turn an enemy flank, this appears to have been achieved only once and there was a disturbing propensity for frontal attacks.[5]

General Talia ad-Duri's 9th Arm Div had mixed fortunes after it crossed the border supported by 12th Arm Bde/3rd Arm Div and 31st SF Bde. The 12th Arm Bde cleared the way through a 30km sweep which isolated a fortified IRIAF command and control facility, then ad-Duri's two armoured brigades drove along the Karkheh to take both Bostan and Susangerd without a fight on 28 September. Susangerd, a small provincial town 40km north-west of Ahvaz, had a population of some 20,000 and lies in rolling territory, but was a minor prize whose only value was that it controlled a bridge over a tributary of the River Karkheh. Ad-Duri lacked infantry to hold the town, which he then abandoned but covered with a chain of observation posts in an

Iranian naval commandos with a jeep mounting a 106mm M40 recoilless gun, inside Khorramshahr, in October 1980. The Iranian Navy's SBS unit and Marines played a major, yet little recognized role in defending Khorramshahr for 35 days in October and November 1980. Apart from fighting, they often ran training courses for the local population and Pasdaran. (Farzin Nadimi Collection)

Survivors from Task Force 37, posing in front of one of their M47Ms. The unit deployed six of these obsolete tanks (and five M60s) to counter the major Iraqi armoured thrust into northern Khuzestan. Exhaustion and heavy wear are clearly visible, not only on their vehicle but on faces and uniforms too. (Tom Cooper Collection)

Despite its cautious advance, the Iraqi Army took a steady toll of casualties from Iranian snipers and ATGM-teams. Here we see the evacuation of several wounded crew members of a BMP-1. (Albert Grandolini Collection)

arc to the west and south while he renewed his advance upon Ahvaz.

By 5 October, the Iraqis finally managed to cross the Karkheh Kur at three locations and secure a 10km-wide bridgehead, but progress eastwards was slow as Iranian resistance increased and 9th Arm Div's supply lines were not only stretched, but were also heavily struck by the IRIAF. By mid-October, the advance was held some 40km south-west of Ahvaz by defenders who consisted largely of Pasdaran augmented by two under-strength companies (one tank and one mechanized) and two self-propelled batteries (M109, M107) from the 92nd IRIA Arm Div's 3rd Bde, whose main body was concentrated around Ahvaz. By mid-November, the Iranians had established a firm line on the southern bank of the Karkheh anchored on Susangerd, which lay like a boil near the Iraqi supply lines and which Talia al-Duri now sought to lance. He sent 35th and 43rd Arm Bdes to retake the town, defended by 400 IIG and Pasdaran, leaving 14th Mech Bde to mask Ahvaz. The attack began on 13 November but took three days to take the town and several Iraqi tanks were lost.

Meanwhile, IRIA engineers helped the local power company to flood first the Karkheh and later Karkheh Kur valleys by breaking the banks and opening sluices.[6] Later, the Iranians flew visitors over the site, where some 150 armoured vehicles were reported still covered by water with their turrets sticking out.[7] Meanwhile, Iranian ground forces, helicopter gunships and IRIAF intensively interdicted enemy supply columns and Tehran assembled some 2,000 Pasdaran and IRIA troops, including an armoured battalion of 92nd IRIA Div, at Hamidiyeh to recapture Susangerd. Many of the Pasdaran had previously been fighting a counter-insurgency campaign in the northern mountains of Kurdistan and found it hard to adjust to conventional warfare in open terrain. Some found themselves under shellfire for the first time, and one commander later commented, 'When this war was imposed on us, we moved from stage to stage with lots of hardship.'[8]

The Iraqis had only hours to enjoy their success, for at dawn on 17 November the Iranian counter-attack struck along the southern bank of the Karkheh to retake Susangerd by the end of the day, supported by some 25 tactical fighter sorties. Not only did the Iranians regain Susangerd, but they also drove a wedge between the two Iraqi brigades to take Hoveyzeh and cut 9th Arm Div's direct communications to the west. The Iraqis tried desperately to retake the village, but by 21 November it was firmly in Iranian hands.

BATTLE OF SHALAMCHEH

By late November, 9th Arm Div controlled an arc south-west of Ahvaz and Operations Chief Asadi was considering a new assault upon Ahvaz with Talia ad-Duri's division reinforced by 20th Mech Bde/5th Mech Div and 3rd Arm Div's 8th Mech Bde. Flooding caused a shortage of drinking water, and while 20th Bde drew some from the Karkheh, much of it had to be brought in from Basra as work began on boring artesian wells. IRIA gunners maintained sustained and accurate fire, which further encouraged Saddam's troops to dig in and became such a problem that Asadi asked the 5th Mech Div commander, Brigadier General Salah Al Qadhi, to consider a helicopter assault upon enemy batteries.[9]

On III Corps' right flank, Qadhi's 5th Mech Div had the key role of the campaign, which was to secure the Shatt's northern bank, then extend Iraqi control up the Karun to Ahvaz, where it would link with 9th Arm Div. His forces here advanced on two narrow axes split by a flooded anti-armour feature dubbed the Fish Lake (Buhayrat Al-Asmak), with 15th Mech Bde advancing from al Qurnah between the Hawizah Marshes and the lake. It crossed the frontier and easily reached the Khorramshahr-Ahvaz highway despite light resistance from an under-strength tank company, two mechanized companies of 3rd Bde/92nd IRIA Arm Div supported by a battalion of 22 M109 and two batteries of 10 M107. It took three days to advance some 50km to Hamid, from where it made contact with 9th Arm Div while still 30km from Ahvaz.[10]

In Basra, Qadhi concentrated 26 AB and 20 MB from 9 September, as engineers threw a 390-metre Soviet-built PMP pontoon bridge

4: THE INVASION OF KHUZESTAN

Although suspected by many Western observers of being grounded, the IRIAA rushed its AH-1 Cobras into combat right from the start of the war. Together with Northrop F-5 Tiger II fighter-bombers from Tactical Fighter Base 4 (TFB.4), Iranian helicopter gunships played a crucial role in the defence of Dezful. (Tom Cooper Collection)

An F-5E Tiger II from the TFB.4, underway at low altitude. Flying up to 60 close air support sorties a day, the three squadrons based at Vahdati AB near Dezful smashed the Iraqi advance toward that town. (Farzin Nadimi Collection)

Troops of the Iraqi 6th Armoured Brigade on the morning of 11 October 1980, waiting for the order to advance using two PMP pontoon bridges constructed over the Karoun River, near Mared. This operation was intended to become a springboard for capturing Abadan. (Tom Cooper Colleection)

(with a carrying capacity of 60 tonnes) across the Tigris with what US intelligence described as 'considerable skill'. Iraqi river-crossing equipment inventory included the GSP ferry system (carrying capacity 52 tonnes), the 40-metre TMM truck-launched bridges (capacity 60 tonnes), the TPP heavy pontoon bridge which could carry up to 70 tonnes in the 185-metre version and PTS tracked amphibious trucks with 10 tonnes capacity.[11]

Fire support came from artillery and MLRS batteries east of Basra, while on the south bank of the Shatt, opposite Khorramshahr and Abadan, was an 18-gun battalion and 160mm mortar batteries. They were augmented by 140mm MLRS in two of the Iraqi Navy's Polish-built Polnocny-D (Project 773) class medium landing ships which were being refitted in Basra when the war broke out, and each ship's pair of launchers could easily reach the north bank of the Shatt.[12] The batteries were protected by air defence assets ranging from ZSU-23-4 self-propelled quad 23mm guns to 2K12 Kub (Cube) (ASCC code SA-6 Gainful) self-propelled triple-missile launchers organized into brigades with 3rd, 6th and 10th Arm Divs, supported by the 155th, 162nd and 175th Missile Brigades respectively.[13]

By 15 September, the Iranians could see enemy armour assembling at the border near Shalamcheh, and as word filtered eastwards the border guards were augmented by a ragtag group of individuals including Marines, some Pasdaran and a few people calling themselves Fadaeiyan-e Islam (Devotees of Islam). Most were killed fighting 26th Arm Bde as it advanced upon Shalamcheh, where the advance was briefly held as Pasdaran, with little ammunition, defended a demolished bridge before being overwhelmed. Most survivors, short of food which they scavenged from abandoned shops, sometimes leaving payment, retreated to Khorramshahr, although some

27

fought as guerrillas in Shalamcheh until they were killed.¹⁴ Militia reinforcements arrived to a very confused and fluid battlefield. An Iranian history notes that a force of Isfahan Basij arriving on the battlefield by bus did not realize they had reached the Forward Edge of Battle Area (FEBA) until they came under fire and later came across the remnants of another convoy which had been destroyed.¹⁵

The hard-working Iraqi engineer corps quickly replaced the Shalamcheh bridge and the advance continued, joined by 3rd Arm Div (Brigadier General Kaddoori Jabiar Al-Duri), which would isolate Khorramshahr from the north. The division's 12th Arm Bde was with 9th Arm Div, while three artillery battalions were in the corps reserve. Recognizing the severity of the threat, the IRIAF directed considerable effort against the enemy advance and helped to restrict progress, so it took the Iraqis three or four days to advance the 15km from the border, cut the main road north to Ahvaz and reach the northern outskirts of Khorramshahr. Iraqi Gazelle helicopter gunships with HOT anti-armour missiles were also active on the Khuzestan front and claimed 17 Chieftains during 1980.¹⁶ With the Iranian government still suspicious of the IRIA, Tehran was forced to transfer operational command in the south to the IIG, with headquarters at Arvand Kenar, although the Gendermerie commanders were unsuitable for conventional military operations

BATTLES OF KHORRAMSHAHR AND ABADAN

Khorramshahr was once Khuzestan's capital and was now the southern terminus of the north-south rail line. Under the Shah, from 1965 it became a city of 270,000, although most of the women, children and elderly were evacuated on 25 September. The city is 7km long and 5km wide and sits at the confluence of the Karun and the Shatt, with part on the Karun's south bank linked by the Basra-Abadan highway bridge some 2.5km upstream.¹⁷ The highway runs west-north-west to east-south-east, with most of the modern city, including the Grand Mosque and police station, to the north, and some 500 metres south of these two buildings there is a roundabout, from which the highway runs straight to the bridge.

Between the highway, the Shatt and the Karun, lies of the heart of the city with the rail station in the north-west and palm groves along the Shatt. Where the waterways meet are the port and oil terminal, with rows of jetties, wharves, quays, a maze of oil pipelines, as well as the customs area with warehouses and storage yards. To the east, sprawling along the Karun's northern bank, was the old town, up to 2km long and 1.5km deep, a maze of twisting streets and alleyways. The north and west was a substantial suburban sprawl following the expansion of the population in the previous decade, while across the bridge the city gradually merged with Abadan to create a single urban area. The outskirts consisted of single-storey brick or mud-brick buildings, often with small gardens, while the centre was dominated by modern, multi-storey buildings.

The IRIA garrison from 92nd Div consisted of only 500 men from the 151st Fortress Btn and elements of 3rd Bde, for the Army realised the city was too exposed and could not be held for long. The only other regular troops present were an under-strength marine battalion reinforced by cadets from the naval base. However, volunteers had rushed to the city's defence and there would be 3,000 fighters, Pasdaran, police, customs officials, Basij and ordinary civilians directed by Pasdaran commander Mohamad Ali Jahanara from the Grand Mosque. The twisting streets of the old town were blocked with barricades, while trenches were dug elsewhere and the handful of

Having crossed the Karoun, Iraqi infantry tried in vain to fight their way into Abadan. These troops are taking cover behind an embankment, supported by an RPG-gunner and a machine-gunner. (Albert Grandolini Collection)

mortars were carefully emplaced. Although ammunition might have been a problem in the long run, the defenders had a plentiful supply of both food and water.¹⁸

The western approaches to the town were shielded by two berms, earth or sand walls created from the earth of a ditch in front of it. With modern earth-moving equipment, they were easy to construct, especially in deserts, to provide an obstacle to vehicle movement. They were thick enough to shelter infantry in foxholes and slit trenches just beyond the crest or immediately behind. The first berm was reportedly held largely by IRIA troops, while the second, some 5km behind it, had militias, together with heavy weapons and some Chieftain tanks, allegedly with orders to shoot the regulars if they attempted to withdraw.

With Saddam's attention focussed upon Abadan and Ahvaz, the Iraqis wished to avoid a prolonged urban battle for Khorramshahr. Indeed, on 1 October, Saddam said he wanted to 'take over the land not the city', which was to be destroyed.¹⁹ Qadhi was to push into the city from the west with 26th Arm Bde, while 3rd Arm Div (Jabiar Al-Duri) isolated it, then push 6th Arm Bde through its northern suburbs to take the highway bridge. He would then advance to Abadan while Qadhi covered his left as Khorramshahr was mopped up and occupied by Special Forces and Popular Army troops. A fast-moving mechanized force might have achieved this, but Jabiar Al-Duri was too slow, and

A dug-in T-62M of the 3rd Armoured Division against a backdrop of a palm grove, near Shatt al-Arab, while preparing to support another push on Khorramshahr. (Albert Grandolini Collection)

as he entered the city's northern and eastern suburbs resistance was stiffening. He was soon under fire from all sides, but desperately decided to press on as the battle for Khorramshahr, like Topsy in Uncle Tom's Cabin, 'just growed'.

The Iraqis' first task was to take the berms, and from 26 September Khorramshahr endured two days of artillery, rocket and mortar fire from the west and across the Shatt. The berms were then assaulted after a separate bombardment and quickly fell, most of the IRIA defenders being lost, and by the night of 29/30 September Jabiar Al-Duri had isolated Khorramshahr. But as he and Qadhi pushed into the suburbs, they suffered losses in a string of ambushes which cost them men and vehicles. The urban environment was ideal for the untrained defenders, for AFVs are vulnerable to short-range anti-armour weapons, which included RPG-7s and US M-40 106mm recoilless rifles with their tracer-equipped spotting rifles, as well as Molotov cocktails. The defenders' few Chieftain MBTs acted as mobile anti-tank guns to dominate open areas and pick off enemy armour.

Infantry from either the 3rd Armoured or 5th Mechanized Division cautiously combing tall grass along the bank of Karoun, while moving towards Khorramshahr. (Albert Grandolini Collection)

The intensity of the resistance was an unpleasant surprise for the Iraqis and underlined a significant weakness, for while 3rd Arm Div had plenty of AFVs and artillery support, it lacked infantry, with no more than 2,5003,000 men available. As the invaders paused to take stock, the IRIA appeared to change its mind about defending the town for, on 1 October, troops from 55th Air Bde were brought in by helicopter, while Iranian artillery fire increased in intensity in the enemy rear.

Despite the earlier setback, Qadhi began pushing into the western edges of the city, relying upon artillery to clear the way, but the rubble restricted AFV movement and provided concealment and shelter for the defenders. Reinforced by two mechanized rifle battalions and elements of the 33rd SF Bde (initially only 8th Btn), but still relying upon their tanks and ICVs, Iraqi spearheads, preceded by rolling barrages, reached the rail station. Some troops may have benefitted from hasty training in an unconventional warfare training complex being built at Salam Pak, some 25km south-east of Baghdad, although it was not completed until February 1981.[20]

The fierce resistance of Iranian Army regulars and various local militias infuriated the invading Iraqis. This is clearly obvious from the ill-treatment of both military and civilian prisoners by this crew of an OT-62. (Albert Grandolini Collection)

Artillery support proved a major problem for the Iraqis. A shortage of airburst fuses for 130mm guns led Shanshal to order Field Artillery Director Major General Salim Bakr to transfer a battery of retired British 87mm gun-howitzers (25 pdrs) from the artillery school to the Khorramshahr front. The BM-21 MLRS provided some compensation and the front had priority for these rockets.[21]

Firepower gradually pushed back the defenders and allowed the Iraqis to establish a command post, protected by T-62 and T-55 tanks, in a fertilizer factory and free part of 5th Mech Div. By 3 October,

When commandos, armour and artillery proved insufficient, the Iraqis rushed some of their 100 ERC-TH (Haut subsonique Otpiquement Teleguide tire d'un tube) armoured cars armed with HOT ATGMs to the front line around Abadan. This vehicle is crossing the Karoun River. (Albert Grandolini Collection)

The ruins of Khorramshahr made an ideal defensive terrain for the Iranians whether regulars from the IRIA, surviving Gendarmes, the Police or the Pasdaran. One of the latter is seen here crouching in the road with his G-3 rifle at the ready. (Albert Grandolini Collection)

they controlled most of the customs areas in the west, but not the port, and were probing the old town, where conditions were ideal for the lightly armed defenders. The battlefield became covered with dense and acrid clouds of black smoke from the blazing oil storage tanks on Abadan, retaliatory bombardments of Iraqi facilities and ships in the Shatt deliberately shelled or caught in the crossfire. Iranian bombardment of the refinery on the Faw Peninsula forced the Iraqis to evacuate the 70,000 civilian population from Faw town, while many of Abadan's 300,000 civilians fled northwards.

During 3 October, the Iraqis tried to advance from the northern part of the customs area to the main road, and from there to the bridge, but encountered the usual fierce resistance, which left 15 AFVs destroyed, including five tanks. Whenever an Iraqi advance was held, the invaders were given no respite and faced frequent counter-attacks, sometimes supported by armour, while police units used tear gas and irritant agents.[22]. Artillery fire usually broke up these attacks, but exploiting the success was difficult, especially in the old town, where the narrow streets, often barricaded, restricted AFV movement, while sniper fire took its toll of the infantry.

The apparent lack of support from IRIA forces, notably the headquarters of 1st Bde/92nd Arm Div, reinforced Pasdaran paranoia as the defenders ran short of heavy weapons, ammunition and even men. The brigade had only its 165th Mechanized Infantry Btn, augmented from the divisional reserve by an artillery battalion (M109) and the Chieftains of 232nd Arm Btn, all of these units at half strength, scattered over a 110km front between Ahvaz and Abadan and in no condition to stage a counteroffensive.[23] The IRIAF began striking supply dumps, gun positions and communications, but on 6 October the Iraqis, now with 12 Arm Bde and reinforced the next day by nine batteries (32 guns), secured the northern suburbs and the western part of the port. The port's eastern part remained firmly in the defenders' hands, together with the old town and bridge, but Iraqi tanks along the waterfront enfiladed streets which ran parallel to the river.

Ni'ami belatedly realized he was no nearer taking Abadan and would need a new approach at Khorramshahr. He was sent reinforcements, augmented from 2 October by new engineer units, as he prepared to go around Khorramshahr, while three days later his artillery began to interdict the east bank highway to Ahvaz. Pressure upon Khorramshahr continued, and from 7 October, as Ni'ami appears to have taken tactical control of storming the city, the Iraqis pushed into both the eastern docks and the old town, remorselessly advancing block by block in three days of bloody fighting. They benefitted from special forces reinforcements, so there were now four battalions (2,000 men) from the 33rd SF Bde, as well as the 3rd Republican Guards Btn (500 men), who were better trained than the average conscript and both self-reliant and flexible in their approach. But there had also been hasty retraining of the infantry in combined arms and urban warfare tactics, as well as night operations.

On 11 October, the 3rd Arm Div by now reinforced by up to six infantry battalions, including from II Corps 49th Bde/11th Inf Div and 23rd Bde/8th Inf Div, as well as two Popular Army battalions with a total strength of some 5,000 men was ready to complete the capture of Khorramshahr, having established a bridgehead across the Karun some hours earlier (see below). Within the city there was a drive southwards into the old town, which a mechanized battalion tried to roll up from the east by pushing along the bank as commandos advanced upon the highway bridge. This took Jahanara by surprise but he reacted quickly, aided by the Iraqis' usual caution, and the advance was quickly stopped.

On 12 October, Iraqi special forces took the bridge but another four days were required to eliminate the defenders around the structure and its northern approaches. With the old town now isolated, the Iraqis began to crush the remaining resistance with increased fire support from across the Shatt, where Ni'ami had added another artillery battalion and mortar batteries. By 24 October, he had taken the whole of Khorramshahr north of the river and established a bridgehead south of the bridge, but the Iranians stopped every Iraqi attempt to break out.

After a brief pause, the Iraqis began a last effort to take the remainder of the city with a new bombardment from 24 October which was so heavy the Iranians complained they could not evacuate their wounded in ambulances.[24] The remaining Iranian Chieftain tanks were unable to contribute much to the defence because the narrow streets limited their fields of fire. During the next two days, the Iraqis tightened their grip and on the night of 25/26 October, most of the defenders, including Jahanara, slipped away to join the defence of Abadan, leaving a wrecked city. The Iranians only acknowledged the loss of

Two Pasdaran inside a wrecked building in Khorramshahr. With their excellent knowledge of local buildings and streets, the Iranians were in possession of a significant advantage, even when fighting Iraqi commando units. (Albert Grandolini Collection)

Two Iranian SBS-commandos who helped defend Khorramshahr, during a lull in fighting on 19 October 1980. (Farzin Nadimi Collection)

the city on 30 October, when batteries on Abadan Island began laying down bombardments on its battered streets. The victors looted the city and sometimes fought among themselves for the spoils, a reaction to their heavy losses estimated at between 4,000 (1,000 dead) to 12,000 (4,000 dead) and up to 100 AFVs; little wonder both sides later referred to the city as Khooninshahr, Khuninistan or 'City of Blood'.[25]

Even as the bloody battle for Khorramshahr raged on, Ni'ami prepared to advance upon Abadan to secure the north bank of the Shatt. But this seemed likely to be as great a hazard as Khorramshahr.

Abadan is effectively a 155km^2 island, with the Shatt curling round to the west and south, the Karun to the north and the Bahmanshir (also written as Bahamshehr) in the east. The Musa Marshes to the north and east extend some 5km north of Abadan's suburbs, while to the north is a dusty plain which is subject to flooding during the rainy season. It is a modern city with a huge oil refinery with storage tank 'farm' at its heart, with most of the homes being to the east.

Abadan faced a heavy bombardment, which included FROG missiles, directed from an observation post across the Shatt near the tiny Iraqi port of Siba. The bombardment was a trial for the defenders, and Iraqi COMINT intercepted a stream of complaints demanding action to relieve their suffering. The garrison was a mechanized battalion, a tank battalion (probably with only 25 tanks), the local IIG regiment, a naval battle group based upon the two Marine battalions and Pasdaran; indeed half the 7,000 defenders were the Islamic Revolution's bearded warriors.[26] They were placed under 2nd Bde/77th IRIA Inf Div, which was gradually transferred from Mashad over a six-week period from late September with some of its component units.[27]

Unable to take the highway bridge in Khorramshahr, Ni'ami decided to launch an amphibious assault north of the city. On 5 October, he received pontoon and ferry companies as political pressure grew, Defence Minister Khairrallah bombarding his headquarters for nearly a fortnight urging him to hurry, while a visit from Shanshal added pressure. Khairrallah proposed using Mil Mi 6 (ASCC code name Hook) heavy helicopters to carry vehicles across the Karun and the reinforcement of 3rd Arm Div with Popular Army units.[28]

With most of 3rd Arm Div in Khorramshahr and the remainder of III Corps fully committed, Saddam decided to leave Jabiar Al-Duri in overall command of crossing the Karun, but augment his forces with elements of 5th Mech Div and II Corps. Shanshal had planned to use Khazraji's 7th Mtn Div, which began practising river crossings, but this was replaced by 8th Inf Div's 23rd Bde, together with 5th Mech Div's 26th Arm Bde which would provide flank cover.[29]

The crossing point was to be near Mared, some 15km north-east of Khorramshahr, where there was firm ground for armour. Jabiar Al-Duri's plan called for 23rd Bde, led by special forces, to storm the opposite bank and establish a bridgehead using GSP ferries, then his engineers would deploy two PMP bridges for 6th Arm Bde. Because the Musa Marshes restricted exploitation eastward, with only the highways north to Ahvaz and east to Bandar-e Khomeini/Bandar-e Mashur being suitable for armour, these meeting just north of Abadan, 6th Arm Bde would seize this junction and advance along the highways as far as possible to isolate Abadan from the north. The defence was weak and was further undermined when 92nd IRIA Div's 232nd Arm Btn simply provided a screen of tank platoons along the bank of the Karun.

The crossing began on the night 10/11 October when there was limited visibility, but it was aided by a 1.5-metre drop in water level during the previous two days. However, a 20-metre band of soft mud on either side meant a considerable amount of preparation work before bridging the river. First, infantry crossed in assault boats to clear the river bank and captured 10 Chieftain MBTs, virtually annihilating the armoured detachment. This was the Iraqi Army's first forced river crossing and the 23rd Bde's heart was not in the mission, with the men unhappy fighting in swampy terrain against aggressive enemy infantry. When enemy pressure forced one battalion commander to adjust his lines by pulling back his lead company, this panicked the rest, who believed it was withdrawing, and while the panic was eventually stopped, it meant the bridgehead was smaller than planned. Meanwhile, Iraqi engineers began assembling the PMPs, but 6th Arm Bde failed to arrive on time, so at dawn work ceased while both equipment and vehicles were camouflaged to avoid IRIAF detection. Iraqi errors actually helped their operation, for they convinced the defenders it was either just a raid or a reconnaissance.

During the day, 6th Arm Bde arrived, and from dusk the PMPs were assembled and most of the armour crossed to assemble upon the eastern bank on 14 October, as 26th Bde moved in behind it to cover its

One of the 624 Chieftain Mk. 5/3P MBTs purchased by Iran from the United Kingdom in the 1970s. All Iranian Ground Forces vehicles of the 1970s and early 1980s were painted in the same light olive green colour, similar to that used by the Israeli Defence Force. National markings consisted of small roundels, usually applied on storage boxes around the turret. The vehicle number (usually consisting of four digits, but in this case limited to '146') was applied in black on turret sides, the front and the rear of the hull. The so-called 'Onion' the stylized word 'Allah', the official crest of the Islamic Republic of Iran was frequently added on skirts, sometimes in the form of a stencil and in red, as shown here, but at least as often applied rather crudely with a brush.

One of 460 M60A1s acquired by Iran from the US during the 1960s. They wore the same standardized colours and national markings as applied on all other Iranian Army vehicles of that time, though apparently without any hull numbers. Nearly all had a Shi'a call for the 12th Imam painted on their turrets too: this was the Arabic inscription 'Ya Qaem-e al-e Mohammad' (meaning 'I call up you the [still alive] hidden member of the Mohammad's family').

The Iranian Army acquired about 300 M113A1 and M113A2 APCs for its armoured divisions in the 1970s, but for most of the war with Iraq these served instead with reconnaissance battalions of various divisions. All were painted in standardized colours, and most received various kinds of inscriptions on their hull sides (and different forms of storage baskets, usually on their hull-fronts). In this case, the inscriptions included hull number '29' in red and 'Allah o-Akbar' ('God is great') in white.

Iraq had only 155 T-72s at the start of the war, all of them assigned to the 10th Armoured Brigade. Most were built in 1975. Although severely cramped, tending to overheat and equipped with a poor fire-control system, they proved much more reliable and capable of outclassing the Chieftain on the battlefield. While some of these early Iraqi T-72s were left in the olive green colour applied before delivery, at least some received the standardized Iraqi Army camouflage pattern consisting of yellow sand and blue-green, shown here. Most have received turret-numbers too (shown here is the example '12'), usually applied in white.

About 1,300 T-62s formed the primary armament of Iraqi armoured divisions at the start of the war. Although their 115mm smoothbore guns were also designed to fire 9M117 Shenska (AT-10 Stabber) ATGMs, the Iraqis received only shells. The type proved not only cramped, but also very vulnerable to any kind of combat damage (even a glancing hit on the front hull could cause internally stored ammunition to detonate), and rapidly overheated the crew during any kind of engagement. Most of the Iraqi T-62s were painted in a standardized camouflage pattern consisting of yellow-sand, with wide stripes of blue-green applied down their sides. Identification insignia (in this case a square of orange, with a vertical blue line) were usually applied on turret sides (next to the turret number, '127' in this case), but often on the fume extractor too.

The general appearance of Iraqi Army T-54/-55s early in the war was similar to that of all other vehicles operated by the service: a camouflage pattern consisting of yellow-sand, with wide stripes of blue-green applied almost vertically down the front and sides. Turret insignia was applied in a number of ways, apparently depending on the unit in question. In this case, it consists of the letter 'J' (standing for 'Jaysh', or 'Army') and the digits '24'. Turret top and sides, and the rear deck, were often crammed full with the crew's personal belongings, but also water cans and machine-gun ammunition.

The principal APC of Iraqi armoured and mechanized formations early in the war with Iran was the OT-62 a Czechoslovak-manufactured BTR-50. Although seldom armed, the type proved reliable and quite popular in service. It could carry up to 20 fully armed troops, and had amphibious capabilities. While few examples were left in the olive green colour applied before delivery, most were camouflaged in standard colours consisting of yellow-sand and blue-green.

Intensive service use and weather conspired to literally disintegrate the camouflage pattern of most Iraqi vehicles within weeks of the start of the war with Iran. This OT-62 survived long enough to receive a small splotch of blue-green on which the hull number ('122') was applied. The rear deck was usually crammed full with personal belongings of the crew though sometimes, as illustrated here, used to carry additional fuel cells taken from some T-54 or T-55 MBTs.

Although armed with a 14.5mm KPVT machine gun and capable of carrying up to 16 fully armed troops, BTR-60s of the Iraqi Army were at least as often used to transport unit staff instead. Their usual camouflage consisted of yellow-sand and blue-green, often applied in near-vertical stripes down the hull, but sometimes in irregular splotches instead.

Although Iraq imported 620 BMP-1s during the 1970s, the type was still relatively rare and usually reserved for crack armoured units, like the 10th Armoured Brigade or 3rd Armoured Division. Most vehicles were camouflaged as shown here: in yellow-sand overall, with near-vertical stripes of blue-green. Many carried various unit insignia or codes on their hull, or turret-sides as shown here, but exact details of the system remain unknown.

A reconstruction of another Iraqi Army BMP-1 sighted early during the war with Iran, somewhere in the Khorramshahr area. As usual, the vehicle is camouflaged in yellow-sand and blue-green, but meanwhile covered by quite a thick layer of sand. The inscription on the turret reads 'J43', with 'J' usually standing for 'Jaysh' ('Army').

Short-range air defence of all mobile formations of the Iraqi Army was the job of the Zenitnaya Aamokhodnaya Ustanovka (ZSU) -23-4 Shilka: a vehicle with four 23mm 2A7 cannons capable of firing up to 4,000 rounds per minute. Fire-control was provided by an RPK-2 (1RL33) radar working in J-band, at a frequency between 10 and 20 GHz. This could detect aircraft and helicopters out to a range of 20km, but its performance was generally degraded by ground clutter. While some Iraqi Shilkas were left in the olive green colour applied before delivery, at least a few received the standard camouflage pattern consisting of yellow-sand and blue-green. None are known to have worn any kind of national or unit insignia.

Iran acquired 214 Bell 206As and Bell 206A-1s in three large batches during the 1970s, at least 12 of which went to the air force, a few to the Navy, while the rest served with the IIAA and then the IRIAA. Painted in dark yellow-sand and dark earth over, and pale grey under, they received serials in the range 2-4101 up to 2-4284. Bell 206A-1s could be armed with a General Electric GAU-2B/A 7.62mm Minigun, mounted on a pylon protruding through the side of the rear cabin, where ammunition was also stored. Inset is the official patch of the Imperial Iranian Army Aviation, applied on all of its helicopters in the 1970s: although largely removed by 1980, some IRIAA aircraft went into the war against Iraq still wearing this patch on their sides. The last two or three digits of the serial number were often repeated on the nose.

No less than 296 Bell 214As – a variant specially developed and built for Iran – were acquired by the IIAA during the 1970s, and locally designated Esfahan. All were painted in dark yellow-sand and dark earth over, and pale grey under. The first batch received serial numbers 6-4651 through to 3-4937, the second 2-6003 to 2-6008. The IIAA patch was usually worn on cockpit doors during the 1970s, but generally replaced by the 'Onion' after the revolution of 1979. Service title – originally IIAA, but extended to IRIAA after 1979 – was usually applied on cabin doors, often in white. As illustrated here, Iranian Bell 214As could be armed – usually with LAU-3/A or similar launchers for 3.75in unguided rockets – but are not known to have applied this configuration during the war with Iraq.

The IIAA received a total of 202 AH-1Js, about 190 of which were available when Iraq invaded Iran. The first 140 of these were delivered with standard armament consisting of the 20mm gun and standard wing stores. But three of these, and subsequently 62 examples, were modified to the full configuration compatible with BGM-71 TOW ATGMs. All were painted in dark yellow-sand and dark earth over, and pale grey under. With much of the Iranian military demobilized and then mauled by purges of commanding officers, the IRIAA struggled to mobilize in reaction to the Iraqi invasion. Many of its helicopters were rushed into combat with incomplete service titles: the first 'I' – standing for 'Imperial' – and the IIAA patch were crudely removed, and only 'IAA' left in its place.

The first armed helicopters in Iraqi service were about 50 Aerospatiale SE.316C Alouette III, acquired in several irregular batches during the 1970s. Most went to the Iraqi Army Aviation Corps when this was established in 1980, and they saw intensive service early during the war with Iran often armed with AS.12 ATGMs or launchers for unguided rockets. All wore a standardized camouflage pattern consisting of sand, mauve and dark green over, and light blue under, and had a large Iraqi national flag on the fuselage. Serials known examples are 1076 (shown here), 1214 and 1298 were applied with a brush on the boom.

The IrAAC inherited a large fleet of about 200 Mi-8Ts and Mi-17s from the IrAF in 1980. Most Mi-8Ts were acquired in the early 1970s, and left in olive green over and light admiralty grey (BS381C/697 or FS35622) on undersides. Serials (here the example serialled as 1268) were left over from the time of their service with the IrAF, applied in order of delivery, and thus anywhere within the range 1200 2100. Applied in black, often with help of stencils, these were worn on the boom. Nearly all wore large national flags applied on the rear cabin sides; some also had two sets of national insignia.

Later during the war with Iran, surviving Mi-8Ts of the IrAAC were overhauled and received a new, standardized camouflage pattern shown here, consisting of sand, dark brown, and dark green on upper surfaces and sides, and light admiralty grey (BS381C/697 or FS35622) on undersides. Their serials were reapplied in European digits, in black, on the boom. Although primarily used for transport and liaison, Iraqi Mi-8Ts were often armed, usually with two or four UB-16-57 or UB-32-57 (shown here) pods for 68mm unguided rockets.

The Iraqis continued rushing their armour into Khorramshahr, even after suffering heavy losses. This T-62 is driving down one of the docks on the northern bank of the Karoun, in the direction of the Old Town. (Albert Grandolini Collection)

One of several Iranian Chieftains knocked out by the Iraqis during the advance on Abadan and Khorramshahr. (Tom Cooper Collection)

flank. The defenders were unaware of the scale of the threat until the afternoon, when a tank battalion of 6th Arm Bde drove up the Ahvaz road and ambushed a convoy coming the other way. Chieftain tanks escorting the convoy covered its hasty retreat, exploiting their superior guns and armour, but both sides were hamstrung by the off-road mud which mired many tanks. The Iranians were driven back and lost a number of AFVs, including at least 20 tanks, as the road came under Iraqi artillery fire, yet it remained a major Iranian artery despite the danger and difficulty. The IRIAF and IRIAA interdicted the bridges, but even when they hit them the modular nature of the PMP made them easy to repair.

Meanwhile, 6th Arm Bde approached Abadan along the eastern bank of the River Bahmanshir. Although harassed by Iranian gunships and leaving a trail of destroyed vehicles, by 16 October it had cut both of the highways to Ahvaz and Bandar-e Khomeini and Bandar-e Mashur to create a bridgehead some 20km deep and 15km wide. But the Iraqis remained within the marsh line and were unable to cut the junction of the two highways to the east, and these became the Abadan garrison's prime supply route. The southern tip of Abadan 'island' was not covered by Iraqi artillery fire, which allowed the Iranians to use small boats, hovercraft and helicopters to ferry reinforcements and supplies, mostly at night, then evacuate the wounded. Some vessels continued to sail into Abadan's naval base, Muhammara, and one was shelled by the newly arrived 49th Inf Bde/11th Inf Div in early October, but when the Iraqi Navy tried to interdict maritime traffic into Abadan it suffered serious losses. The lifelines helped to reinforce the garrison, bringing the defenders to some 10,000, including 5,000 Pasdaran, who were grimly confident of holding the wrecked city, yet they would not be tested too greatly.

The Iraqis sought to tighten their hold on Abadan, and on the night of 31 October/1 November used assault boats to cross the Bahmanshir to the south of Abadan and established a pontoon bridge to support a bridgehead. This bridgehead was slowly expanded in the face of stiff resistance, with numerous counter-attacks, while fixed- and rotary-wing aircraft pounded the Iraqi rear, but, ultimately, it was the Iraqis' lack of infantry which hamstrung their attempt to take Abadan. The front remained extremely open, and early in November, Iranian Oil Minister Muhammad Jawad Baqir and several aides were captured while making an unescorted tour of inspection of the oil fields. He would tell his captors that even ministers were not informed about events on the battlefield.[30]

For 10 days the struggle continued, then the Iranians launched an attack using the 77th IRIA Div's 153rd Inf Btn (Lieutenant Colonel Manuchehr Kehtari), marines and Pasdaran, with helicopter and some fixed-wing air support, and this drove the enemy back across the river by 19 November, their pontoon bridge being destroyed. By now Abadan was under constant tank and artillery bombardment, and to create a jump-off point for a new attack into the town during November, the Iraqis tried to throw another PMP across the Shatt directly into Khorramshahr, but were thwarted by accurate Iranian artillery fire. Nevertheless, the Iraqis were able to strengthen their bridgehead across the Karun and to take more of the road to Bander-e Mahshur and Bandar-e Khomeini, but exhaustion and the weather combined to bring operations against Abadan to a halt by mid-November.[31] US intelligence commented that the two urban battles deprived the Iraqis of 'the psychological, logistical and strategic initiative'.[32] One side effect of the two battles was that the Iranian marines suffered some 90 percent casualties and Tehran disbanded the corps.[33]

THE ARMIES TAKE STOCK

Baghdad had hoped to take Abadan and Khorramshahr by the Islamic festival of Eid al-Adha (Festival of the Sacrifice) on 20 October. But on 19 October, Saddam appeared on television to state that victory had eluded his forces because of 'geographical injustice' and the enemy's technological superiority. During this speech, he referred to the conflict as a 'Jihad' (holy war) which would be second only to the Battle of Qadisiyya. During the third week of November, the rainy season began and lasted until the end of February 1981, washing out the fighting. The rivers flooded and the plains became marshes, effectively isolating many Iraqi formations, but the problem was anticipated and Iraqi engineers had begun to build a network of all-weather roads from Basra towards Ahvaz, and these were used to distribute arms, ammunition and supplies to forward depots.

With fighting reduced to skirmishes and artillery duels, both sides took stock. The Iraqi Army had barely achieved its minimum objectives and failed to take most key urban areas due to excessive caution of specific commanders. Blind firepower replaced well-timed manoeuvre, there was an over-reliance upon armoured/mechanized forces and little attempt at combined arms operations or even of integrating them with air power. Indeed, in stark contrast to the IRIAA, the first time the IrAAC planned and used its helicopter force, according to General Hamdani, was only on 27 October 27.[34] As one commentator noted: "Operationally, the offensive was marred by excessively centralized command and control, poorly chosen objectives, faulty tailoring of forces, ineffective combined arms and lack of joint co-ordination."[35]

Saddam demanded his commanders learn the lessons from their experiences, yet he was responsible for many of the problems, either directly (through centralized command) or indirectly (through his choice of subordinates). With every month, Iran's numerical superiority became a growing threat, with the force ratio dropping from 6:1 in Saddam's favour to 2:1 by November, and soon it would be reversed. This made him acutely aware of casualties, yet while he demanded reductions in casualties, he informed 10th Arm Div commander Major General Hesham Sahah to avoid heavy losses and later complained to his cronies that Sahah needed to be 'educated'. On 7 December 1980, Saddam announced Iraq would confine itself to ambushes, raids and patrols, and that ambushes were to be well-planned, avoid excessive losses and seek a 1:5 casualty rate in Iraq's favour.[36]

Saddam recognized he was in a strategic impasse; his gamble that a swift seizure of terrain would encourage regime change in Tehran had failed, leaving him unable either to advance or retreat. The Iranian regime was in no mood to negotiate, and while unready to launch its own offensives, it certainly would not allow Saddam simply to fold his tent and withdraw. Even if he did, the loss of prestige would probably encourage Shi'a unrest within his own borders, so all he could do was to strengthen his bridgeheads and hope for an opportunity to negotiate control of the Shatt.

In Tehran, the political situation was unsettled, with a struggle for control of the revolution between the secular liberals and leftists on one side and the clerics on the other. For the clerics, the war created a situation beyond their comprehension. They conceived of combat in heroic terms, led by the Pasdaran fighting and dying until they had killed all the hated invaders. IRIA attempts to introduce reality in terms of combined-arms tactics and logistics were regarded, if at all, with suspicion. Yet the situation was not without hope, for the country had a huge numerical advantage in terms of manpower; indeed, so many Iranians volunteered to fight that neither the IRIA nor the Pasdaran could absorb them, and many were sent to eastern Iran on policing and counter-insurgency duties. Many Pasdaran (and Basij) recruits went to the front without weapons to continue the fight with weapons from those killed or wounded, while some IRIA armoured and mechanized units had twice as many men to man their vehicles than they needed, and began rotating their personnel so they spent only one week in four at the front. The IRIA and the regular armed forces were further boosted with the reintroduction of tax privileges for their personnel, both to attract their return to the colours and to boost their morale.[37]

However, there was a shortage of qualified junior leaders, while command and control was further hamstrung, both by a lack of

Chieftains probably from the 232nd Armoured Battalion line up before engaging Iraqi forces that had crossed the Karoun. (Albert Grandolini Collection)

Iraqi troops atop a captured Chieftain, near Susangerd, in late September 1980. The vehicle might have been lost to mechanical failure or because it had run out of fuel. (Albert Grandolini Collection)

Every evening, Iraqi units went into a laager behind earthen berms dug by their engineers. Here, T-55s are moving out to their laager while passing by a bulldozer that spent the afternoon erecting such a protective position. (Albert Grandolini Collection)

radios and the presence of suspicious clerical 'advisors' acting like Soviet Army commissars, ready to meddle in military matters. There remained great tensions between the IRIA and the Pasdaran, whose brave and stubborn defence of urban areas had enhanced

Time and again, Iraqi laagers were exposed to local Iranian counter-attacks. These two T-55s are shown shortly after repelling one such attack (note the spent shell casings on and around the two tanks). Notable are turret markings in the form of small fields in black or blue-green, with the word 'Jaysh' and turret number in white. (Albert Grandolini Collection)

their prestige, although their performance in mobile operations was untested. Bani-Sadr's support for the IRIA was a major source of friction between himself and the clerics, which overshadowed the Iranian response to the invasion.

The IRIA's artillery won the clerics' grudging respect because it proved more than a match for their opponents in terms of accuracy and firepower. Because much Iranian ordnance consisted of self-propelled mountings, they could, in the contemporary jargon, 'shoot and scoot', and were especially effective in a counter-battery role against the less mobile and more exposed Iraqi towed artillery. Saddam's 130mm guns were also running short of ammunition and were increasingly augmented by 122mm M-30 howitzers from the mountain divisions, but by late October 1980 the Iraqis had also fired 40,000 of its 83,000 rounds of 122mm howitzer ammunition.[38]

The 'Achilles heel' of the Iranian forces was logistics, a weakness inherited from the Shah's army. The sophisticated American-developed computer-based inventory system for all the services' logistical organizations was not operational when the revolution broke out, and then 'the Great Satan' took many of the electronic records. It took much time, amid the chaos of revolution and war, to get the system back online, often using manual methods to locate material and then update computer inventories, and the Iranians discovered that poor storage and maintenance techniques had left some material useless.

The loss of many experienced maintenance personnel from the armed forces during the revolution had reduced serviceability rates, especially vehicles and aircraft. While many returned after the invasion, a year's neglect meant much equipment required extensive maintenance and repair, which consumed huge amounts of spares. Abandoned vehicles now had to be recovered for repair, which created backlogs at maintenance centres which were hundreds of kilometres behind the front. This forced the Iranians to cannibalize for spares on a large scale, which provided another hurdle to offensive operations.[39]

Tehran had the advantage of five production facilities, developed by the Shah and producing infantry weapons such as the 7.62mm German G-3 rifle, MG-1 machine gun and RPG-7, 105mm and 155mm shells, 81mm and 120mm mortar bombs, ammunition, propellants, explosives and some communications equipment. There was also a tank repair facility at Masjed-e Soleyman, but this had relied upon foreign supervision, mostly West German and American, and their departure saw production and maintenance capabilities decline.[40]

While the Iraqis also faced logistical problems, their organization remained one of the Army's most efficient elements. US Intelligence would note about 1984 that their logistic and support preparations were 'reasonably competent.'[41] The Iraqis displayed an 'inventive use' of their tank transporter fleet, while the engineer organization was especially effective in building roads and providing bridging.

But unlike Iran, Iraq had made no effort to ease its dependence upon imported defence equipment. It even lacked a small-arms ammunition plant, although it would create small arms and shell production facilities, and initially it depended upon pre-war stocks.[42] The failure of Saddam's 'smash-and-grab' strategy exposed this weakness, which within four months caused serious shortages of all materials, but especially spares and ammunition. The country was dependent upon imports even of fuel, for the IRIAF methodically bombed Petrol Oil and Lubricants (POL) targets to create fuel shortages, overcome only through imports from Kuwait and Saudi Arabia.

Saddam's failure either to consult with, or to warn, the Soviet Union of his intentions provoked fury in Moscow, which was hoping to win influence in Tehran. Indeed, in October 1980, Soviet Minister Vladimir Vinogradov met Iran's Premier, Mohammad Ali Rajai, and Speaker, Hojatolislam Ali Akbar Rafsanjani, to discuss improved relations between the two countries. Between January and September 1980, Iraq received $1.9 billion worth of military equipment, mostly from the Soviet Union, including 300 T-54/55, 700 T-62, 50 T-72, 250 BTR-50, 250 BTR-60PB and 200 BMP-1. An angry Moscow now refused to replace military materiel consumed during the invasion, and some ships were ordered to return to the Soviet Union, including a consignment of 139 T-72 MBTs scheduled to re-equip an armoured brigade which reached the Jordanian port of Aqaba immediately after the invasion.[43] In November 1980, Soviet Communist Party General Secretary Leonid Brezhnev ordered an end to all weapons transfers, while two visits to Moscow by Foreign Minister Tariq Aziz in September and November to secure additional arms shipments were rebuffed, but Poland and East Germany were more venal and received orders for T-54/55 tanks.[44] Only during the spring of 1981, when it was obvious the Iranian theocracy intended to keep the atheist Communists at arm's length, did Moscow change its mind. Yet the Russians would keep open their options, and by 1987 they would supply an estimated $11.8 billion of military equipment to Iran, compared with $43.2 billion to Iraq.[45]

But absorbing equipment proved more difficult for the Iraqi Army

A T-62M from the 3rd Armoured Division cautiously manoeuvring down a street inside Khorramshahr. With the Iranians turning the entire city into a giant minefield, covered by snipers and tank-hunting teams, the Iraqis quickly learned all sorts of lessons about urban warfare. (Albert Grandolini Collection)

A famous photograph of another T-62M from the 3rd Armoured Division, taken in front of the city's Grand Mosque. Note the turret number (12) applied in white, and the crew's sleeping bags and other kit attached behind the hatches. (Albert Grandolini Collection)

than acquiring it, because a shortage of trained manpower forced it to rely upon semi-skilled or even unskilled men, even in armoured units. Neglect and inadequate training was reflected in serious and widespread problems keeping vehicles, and even artillery, working, even though each division had vehicle repair facilities, while there were depots in the rear to repair vehicles, including APCs, and two major repair facilities at Baghdad and Khan al Mahawil for tanks and other equipment.[46] There was much training to overcome the problem, yet units still returned sophisticated equipment, especially electronics and electro-opticals, to depots because they were unable to repair them. Much of this depot work was carried out by foreign technicians, and it appears that a Russian team was largely responsible for maintaining the power packs of the T-72s.[47]

Saddam had to recognize his army was weaker than the enemy in several significant areas. The IRIAF's Phantoms were striking all over Iraq, hitting carefully selected targets. By November 1980, they effectively destroyed the Iraqi oil industry and fuel stocks, causing severe shortages of fuel which forced Baghdad to start importing via Jordan and Kuwait. IRIAA helicopters proved not only superior to those of the IrAAC, but also capable of – in co-operation with a few scattered task forces of the Iranian Army – holding off assaults by entire Iraqi Army corps. In Khuzestan, there was an added problem when the shield against Iranian air attacks was weakened with the withdrawal, in October, of 155th Missile Bde with its Gainful SAMs from the sector under the control of the 3rd Arm Div, because these were necessary for defence of construction site of Iraq's nuclear reactor at Tuwaitha. Iranian artillery was also superior: it not only proved more mobile than that of the Iraqi Army, but longer-ranged too: 18km for the M109A1's 155mm howitzer and 40km for the M107's 175mm gun, allowing them to strike Iraqi rear areas with impunity. By contrast, the Iraqi 122mm M-30 and D-30 howitzers had a range of 11.8 and 15.4km, and the 152mm ML-20 and D-20 gun-howitzers could reach just over 17km, although the 130mm gun had a range of 27.5km.

Anticipating this problem, the Iraqi Army wanted each corps to have an artillery brigade with a battery of 30.4km-range Russian S-23 180mm towed guns. The Russians themselves had produced only a small number of these guns and were reluctant to export them; they even tried to cancel the original Iraqi order for one battery.[48] The Iraqis began to seek their own heavy artillery for counter-battery fire, as well as self-propelled platforms, but this weakness would take a couple of years to overcome. Iraqi artillery support was also undermined by a tendency to break down batteries into two-gun sections, which prevented massed fire, while batteries were stationed too far in the rear to bring down fire on enemy forces. Close air support could not compensate for these weaknesses because there was no direct communication between the units of the two services. The Americans claimed the IrAF leadership was reluctant to commit aircraft for fear of losses, and this was reflected by their pilots, who tended to deliver ordnance prematurely or inaccurately.[49]

The end of the year saw both sides reorganizing in Khuzestan. The Iraqis began building defences, which marked the high tide of their advance and left their forces in positions like flotsam. They built berms behind barbed wire entanglements and minefields, and buttressed them with triangular company positions as the main line of resistance (MLR) with a screen of outposts some 350 metres ahead, and a second berm up to 2km behind, with infantry positions and revetments for AFVs to shelter reserves.[50] A shortage of infantry meant the MLR was very lightly held at first, although flooded areas restricted enemy access in the north. The Iraqis had a mechanized brigade in Khorramshahr, one in the north facing Ahvaz and a third along the Karun. An armoured brigade was south-east of Khorramshahr and a second had moved south-west of Basra, while the Karun bridgehead, supported by a third PMP bridge, had an armoured and a mechanized brigade. III Corps was extending the road network around, and to, Basra, while more pontoon bridges were brought in for major waterways.[51]

The Iranians also improved their communications, and in December threw a pontoon bridge across the Bahmanshir some 5km south-east of Abadan to improve the flow of supplies into the town. This was aided by mobilizing a fleet of trucks, tractor-trailers, vehicle- and barge-mounted cranes as well as enrolling naval helicopters and BH-7 hovercraft. The Iranians also made no attempt to defend in depth, with positions dug on the FEBA to ensure not an inch more of territory was lost and to help their forces reorganize for a riposte, for which they began to launch numerous small raids and made extensive use of their attack helicopters.

Around the enemy Karun bridgehead, and south-east of Abadan, the IRIA augmented the Pasdaran with two tank battalions (66 tanks), a mechanized and an artillery battalions of 92nd Arm Div, together with air defence batteries of ZSU-23-4, although there were

An Iraqi 23mm ZU-23 anti-aircraft gun covering the Shatt al-Arab from Iranian air strikes. Visible in the background are some of the 80 ships from 20 different countries that were trapped in this vital waterway by the Iraqi invasion. (Albert Grandolini Collection)

An Iraqi T-55 on the streets of Khorramshahr, with a soldier from one of the commando units passing by. Soviet-built tanks like this T-55 were cramped, so crews tended to fit all of their personal gear, food, water and ammunition into fittings around the turret. (Albert Grandolini Collection)

also HAWK (MIM-23) surface-to-air missile emplacements near Bandar-e Mahshur. Pasdaran forces flooded into the province, but so did the IRIA, which despatched brigades of the 21st and 37th Inf Divs to support the 92nd Div's 1st and 3rd Bdes, while the 55th Airborne Bde moved down from the Dezful front and on 11 November, the Gendarmerie Khuzestan Command was ordered to relieve Abadan.[52]

It was obvious that the Iranian response could not reply upon a myriad local unco-ordinated organizations, and Ground Forces Headquarters established four forward operations headquarters, including the east at Torbat-e Heydariyeh, the north-west at Urmia (also written Urumiyeh) and the west at Kermanshah. The Southern Forward Operations Headquarters (SFOH), also known as Karbala, was at Ahvaz, split into the Dezful and Khuzestan sectors, and supported by the 22nd and 33rd Artillery Groups, as well as the 2nd and 3rd Area Support Commands for logistics and elements of Transportation and Engineering Commands, the last also responsible for signal groups.[53] The Iranians benefitted from the excellent strategic communications system created by the Shah and based at Lavisan.[54]

Bani-Sadr's grip of military affairs was always uncertain and it was clear that direction of the war effort needed greater co-ordination between the armed forces and the government. Neither Khomeini nor the clerics had any real understanding of military matters and he would later condemn those "who interfere with the armed forces, while being ignorant of military affairs like myself". To improve direction of the war effort, Bani-Sadr visited Khomeini in early October to sanction the revival of the Supreme Defence Council (SDC), established by the Shah and dissolved with his fall. The SDC was created on 13 October 1980 with the president at its head, and had six more members, of whom half were from the armed forces and half were senior clerics, for Khomeini insisted no one side could dominate decision–making.[55]

A major problem which would affect Iran throughout the war was the weakness of the national communications system along the whole front, but especially in Khuzestan. The system ran mostly north-to-south rather than east-to-west, partly because it was designed to support resistance to a Soviet invasion from the north, and this made it difficult to supply the front. The system inevitably came under attack and a Russian source estimated the damage to the Iranian transport network from 1980 to 1985 was worth $4 billion.[56]

Iran had 4,525km of single-track, standard gauge (1.435 metre) rail line, often with weak beds, and most of the main lines ran westwards from Tehran.[57] One ran north-westwards to Van in Turkey and another ran from Qasvin through Qom, Ademeshk (west of Dezful) to Ahvaz and Abadan in Khuzestan through the mountainous terrain, which slowed movement, which could be made only in one direction at a time. The network lacked locomotives and rolling stock, with only 344 of the former and 13,872 freight wagons with a total capacity of 6,347 tonnes, the freight trains being capable of a maximum speed of 55km/h (28mph).[58] The average capacity of the trains was 849 tonnes, of which 365725 tonnes could be moved into Khuzestan.

The Shah augmented this system with an excellent road network consisting of 85,000km of highway, of which 19,000km was 'hard top' (bituminous surface), 36,000km was crushed stone/gravel and the remainder was simple beaten earth.[59] The metalled roads were largely found in the west and south of the country and had two lanes, but the roads were vulnerable to the weather, and both they and the railways in the Zagros Mountains could be blocked by snow, while the winter floods swamped many roads in Khuzestan, although the major routes were usually on embankments.

Although the IRIA was estimated to have some 22,500 US and Russian trucks and 900 MAZ-537 and Faun tank transporters, many of these were unserviceable.[60] This caused a serious shortage of vehicles, which forced Tehran to mobilize civil vehicles, including double-decker buses, but this disrupted the economy, a logistical problem similar to that experienced by the Wehrmacht during Operation Barbarossa, the invasion of Russia. During the war, about half the military supplies were carried in foreign-made civilian vehicles, for which it was difficult to obtain spares, the difficulty made greater by the wide variety of models.[61]. Individual transport owners quickly found ways to make large profits from moving war materiel, while some government officials siphoned off goods for personal gain.[62] Fuel and lubricants for all the forces was also a problem for a country which had lost considerable refining capability; indeed, even in the early twenty-first century it suffered shortages of vehicle fuel, leading to rationing. Because of this inadequate road network, transport aircraft of the IRIAF and IIAC were heavily utilized and in December 1980 moved all the personnel of 88th Arm Bde from Chahbahar to Khuzestan.

While supplies could be shipped to Khuzestan through Bandar-e Khomeini, Bandar-e Mahshur, Bushehr and Bandar Abbas, the ports were severely congested. US intelligence estimated Bandar-e Khomeini (probably including Bandar-e Mashur) had a capacity of 15,000 tonnes per day, but it was so close to the war zone that few merchantmen were willing to sail there. Bandar Abbas had a military capacity of 9,300 tonnes per day, and its civilian port was not yet operational. However, it was 1,600km from Tehran and 950km from the front line. Bushehr was closer to the front but had a capacity of only 3,200 tonnes, and also had a poor transport infrastructure. Increased activity and inadequate loading/unloading facilities meant lengthy delays for ships using the ports, and with only Bandar-e Khomeini having a rail link, all other traffic was by truck.[63]

The Iraqis also had transport problems, beginning with their ports. In normal times, the port of Basra could handle 11,800 tonnes daily, while Um Qasr could unload 4,400 tonnes, but access to Basra was blocked by dozens of derelict foreign merchant ships, which would remain until the end of the war, while fire from each bank of the Shatt further prevented shipping movements.[64]

Consequently, supplies had to come overland. Baghdad's relations with Kuwait and Saudi Arabia to the south were good, but Iranian control of the Straits of Hormuz meant few military supplies could be brought in through the Gulf. Syria had long been a rival of Iraq, and therefore a friend of Iran, despite President Asad's Ba'athist and secular policies, so it not only closed the border but also the oil pipeline from Iraq. Turkey was friendly to both countries and had a common foe in the Kurds, but there were few roads into Iraq through the mountainous frontier and this prevented any substantial movement of military equipment. Fortunately for Saddam, Jordan was a traditional friend of Baghdad, which meant the Red Sea port of Aqaba would become the main conduit of Iraqi military (and civilian) supplies. However, according to a 1985 US Defense Intelligence Agency report, Iraq's primary source for Soviet supplies was Thuwal, near Jeddah, in Saudi Arabia, some 1,800km from Baghdad. The DIA claimed that in 1981 a million tonnes of military supplies were delivered through the Saudi port, which it calls Tuwwal.[65]

Distribution of the supplies was aided by Iraq's two rail lines; one with standard (1.435 metre) gauge and the other with a narrow (1 metre) gauge. The 1,000km standard gauge line was a single track running from Syria down to Basra and Um Qasr, and had 308 diesel locomotives and 8,040 items of rolling stock, including 4,480 freight platforms, of which 400 were flat bed and 457 were for liquids. The 500km narrow gauge line ran north-east from Baghdad to Irbil, and had 77 steam locomotives and a rolling stock inventory of 2,260.[66]

Far more reliance was placed on the road system, which was especially well developed in the east and also across the Jordanian border. The country had 9,000km of 'hard-top' road, with two routes crossing the border into Iran, and 12,000km of gravel or beaten earth road. The Army vehicle fleet could be augmented by some 80,000 civilian trucks and buses, including plenty of heavy trucks and tractor-trailers, to bring supplies up from Aqaba, augmented by Jordanian vehicles. Baghdad also had sufficient storage facilities for 300,000 tonnes of ammunition, but suffered periodic shortages due to its dependency upon imports.[67] While Baghdad faced greater problems importing war materiel than Iran, it had the advantage of interior lines, which made it easier to distribute supplies and equipment at all levels.

Chapter 4 Notes
1. For the Arab uprising in Khuzestan 1979 1980, see Farrokh, p.337; O'Ballance, p.21; Ward, p.233; Zabih, p.15. The Iranian governor at the time was Admiral Ahmad Madani, who would later flee to France.
2. *Saddam's Generals*, pp.30, 32. Others were Brigadier General Hisham al-Fakhri, General Nizar al-Khazraji and Brigadier General Taha Shakarji.
3. UK NA FCO 8/4156.
4. Operations of 1st Mech and 10th Arm Divs will be described in a later publication on the Central and Northern Fronts. Information on 10th Arm Bde from General Makki.
5. For the invasion and northern axis, see Cooper & Bishop, pp. 9091; Farrokh, pp.35254; *Lessons*, pp. 87, 9596; Malovany, pp.13739; O'Ballance, pp.3536, 38, 4041; Pollack, *Arabs*, pp.18693. CRRC SH-PDWN-D-001-021. US AISC, pp. 4.23, 4.27.
6. Buchan, p.338.
7. For the sunken vehicles, see O'Ballance, pp.4041; Hiro, pp.4445.
8. Murray & Woods, p.110, quoting CRRC SH-MISC-D-001-350.
9. CRRC SH-SHTP-D-000-856.
10. For 5th Mech Div's advance on Ahvaz, see Hiro, p41; *Lessons*, p.87; O'Ballance, pp.3537. AISC, pp.4-23, 4-27; Imposed War website.
11. The Iraqis received 45 GSP by 1970, ordered another 200 second-hand units in 1983 and received them the following year. Iraqi armoured and mechanized units also had Russian MTU-20, Czech MT-55KS and East German BLG-60 Armoured Vehicle-Launched Bridges (AVLB). For Iraqi Army water-crossing, see The National Training Center, *The Iraqi Army:Organization and Tactics*, p.150, hereafter NTC *Iraqi Army*.
12. *Saddam's Generals*, pp.9, 160.
13. Information from Tom Cooper.
14. For initial operations along the northern bank, see Nejad, pp.1016; US AISC, p.4-23; Imposed War website.
15. Murray & Woods, p120.
16. Cooper & Bishop, p.85.
17. See Malovany and McLaurin in his monograph, *The Battle of Khorramshahr*, hereafter McLaurin, for excellent sketch maps.
18. For Khorramshahr, see Cooper & Bishop, pp. 96, 10203; Farrokh, p.354; Hiro, pp.41, 4344; *Lessons*, pp. 9294; Malovany, pp.14041, 14548; Marashi & Salama, p.157; McLaurin, pp.2732; Murray & Woods, pp.113, 12022, 124; Nejad, pp.1519; O'Ballance, pp.3738, 40; *Project 1946*, pp.6869; Ward, pp.25152. Lieutenant Colonel R.W. Lamont, 'A Tale of Two Cities – Hue and Khorramshahr', *Armor* magazine; US AISC, pp. 4-28, 4-29, 4-33, Figure 4-10; CRRC SH-MISC-D- 000-827 and SH-SHTP-D-000-856, DIA DDB-1100-343-85, pp.5556, and DDB-2680-103-88, p.19; Imposed War website.
19. CRRC SH-MISC-D-000-827, p.15.
20. Marashi & Salama, p.157; DIA DDB-1100-343-85, p.33.
21. Whether or not the 25 pdrs were sent to this front is unclear. The Iraqis used 25 pdrs and even former British 5.5in (139.7mm) gun howitzers, and during the week 1925 April 1981, these guns fired 806 and 354 rounds respectively. Murray & Woods, Table 5.1.
22. US AISC, pp.4-28, 6-19.
23. Based upon DIA DDB-1100-342-86 and the Imposed War website.

24. Murray & Woods, p.121.
25. The DIA stated 5,000 Iraqis were killed. DDB-1100-343-85, p.56. Jahanara, who would be killed in later fighting, had organized a brave and sustained defence at great cost; one figure quotes 7,000 Iranian casualties; Ward, p.252.
26. The first Abadan Pasdaran unit was the Tarigholgods Btn, which later expanded into the Fathol-Mobin Bde and then the 30th Beit-ol-Moghaddas Div. Zabih, p.156.
27. Davis, *Iranians' Operational Warfighting Ability*, p.7, hereafter, Davis.
28. The Iraqis had six Hooks, capable of carrying a 12-tonne load, and they were used to move jeep-type vehicles and light trucks, as well as supplies, across both the Karun and the Karkheh. Information from Farzin Bishop.
29. For Abadan, see Buchan, p.339; Cooper & Bishop, pp.98, 100; Farrokh, p.360; Hiro, p.43; *Lessons*, pp.9495; Malovany, pp.14850; McLaurin, p.31; Murray & Woods, pp.123, 153; O'Ballance, pp.37, 3940; *Saddam's Generals*, pp.13031; US AISC, pp. 4-28, 4-29, 4-33; CRRC SH-PDWN-D-001-021; DIA DDB-1100-343-85, pp.5556; Imposed War website.
30. Murray & Woods, p.120.
31. US AISC, pp.4-33, 4-34.
32. Op cit, p.4-27.
33. DIA DDB-2680-103-88, p.19.
34. *Project 1946*, p.53.
35. Griffin, p.19.
36. Griffin, p.18; Murray & Woods, pp.126, 12829.
37. McLaurin, p.27; Ward, p.248.
38. Murray & Woods, pp.123, 153.
39. US AISC, pp.4-34, 5-30, 5-32, 5-33.
40. Op cit, p.5-33; US DIA DDB-1100-342-86, pp.2425.
41. For Iraqi logistics, see US AISC, pp.4-43 to 4-45, 5-35.
42. DIA DDB-1100-IZ-81, p.xxi.
43. CRRC SH-MISC-D-000-827, p.35.
44. O'Ballance, p.51; Murray & Woods, p.155; Pelletiere, *The Iran-Iraq War*, p. 44, hereafter Pelletiere. SIPRI yearbooks.
45. See Atkeson's article' Iraq's Arsenal: Tool of Ambition'.
46. DIA DDB-1100-343-85, p.45.
47. Op cit, p.62.
48. The 180mm battery was attached to II Corps, but the Iraqi Army had only 1,400 rounds for it. CRRC SH-SHTP-D-000-856, pp.27, 44.
49. DIA DDB-1100-343-85, pp.89. Saddam was especially critical of IrAF reconnaissance efforts. Murray & Woods, p.119 and f/n 109.
50. Based upon DIA DDB-1100-343-85, pp.5859, Figure 21.
51. US AISC, p.4-34.
52. Cooper & Bishop, p. 94. US AISC, pp.4-34, 4-47, Fig 4-12. Imposed War website.
53. DIA DDB-2680-103-88, p.5, DDB-1100-342-86, pp.14, 22, Figures 12 and 15. The 3rd Area Support Command was transferred from Tehran.
54. DIA DDB-1100-342-86, p.35.
55. Farrokh, p.322; O'Ballance, pp,51, 65; Zabih, p.147. All Refer Country Study and Country guide website: Iran The Revolutionary Period.
56. Davis, p.7, quoting Ye Gromov, 'Principal Iranian Communication Routes and Ground Transportation', *Zarubezhnoye Voyennoye*, No.11 (November 1987), pp.40, 43.
57. For the Iranian rail system ,see Davis, *Iranian … Ability*, pp.67; Goldsack, *Jane's World Railways 19801981*, pp.29091, 484; DIA DDB-1100-IZ-81, DDB-1100-342-86, pp.2325, DDB-2680-103-88, p.14. The DIA calculated Iran had 4,061km of track.
58. The DIA claimed there were 424 locomotives, 4,730 enclosed freight wagons (boxcars), 1,488 open wagons (flatcars) and 2,347 tank wagons for liquids.
59. For the road system, see DIA DDB-2680-103-88, p.14, and DDB-1100-343-85, pp.2325.
60. Truck strength, DIA DDB-2680-103-88, pp.1213.
61. Davis, p.7; Ward, p.263.
62. USAIC, p.5-32.
63. Op cit, p.5-32.
64. DIA DDB-1100-IZ-81, p.xxx.
65. DDB-1100-343-85, p.6.
66. This description of Iraqi communications is based upon DIA DDB-1100-343-85, pp.41, 45, DDB-2680-103-88, p.19, and DDB-1100-IZ-81 pp.xxixxxx; US AISC, pp.5-34, 5-35.
67. DIA DDB-1100-343-85, p.41.

5
The Iranians Strike Back

The need to expel the Iraqi invaders was an issue of personal survival for President Bani-Sadr. Spearheaded by Ayatollah Seyyed Mohammad Hosseini Beheshti's Islamic Republic Party (IRP), the clerics began to isolate him and berated his failure to liberate the occupied territory. This aggravated their paranoia and many suspected him of 'Bonapartist tendencies', fearing he wished to use the IRIA against Khomeini, their fears fed when he temporarily placed the Pasdaran under its command. Khomeini was more tolerant because he and Bani-Sadr had developed a close relationship while sharing their Parisian exile, and continued to urge his followers not to criticize the regular armed forces so vehemently.

The IRP demanded seats on the SDC to control the armed forces, and Bani-Sadr urgently needed a battlefield victory to regain prestige. His allies in the IRIA agreed, but wished to wait until the spring when the ground had dried, for they were aware that much of the IRIA remained committed against the Kurds, there was a shortage of trained staff officers and artillery ammunition, while much of the IRIAA fleet was undergoing maintenance. Yet they had little choice but to begin planning Operation Hoveyzeh (also written as Howeizeh and Hoveize) and supporting operations from 18/20 December.[1]

As diversionary attacks were launched upon the central front around Qasr-e Shirin and Mehran, the Ahvaz-based SFOH would launch three offensives, whose prime objective was to eliminate the Iraqi salient pointing at the city like a dagger. These attacks would be channeled by extensive inundations created by the Iranians to shield the western approaches to Ahvaz, which, together with the seasonal rains, had left much of the battlefield muddy. Operation Hoveyzeh would be launched in the Karkheh and Karkheh Kur valleys to roll up the northern face of the salient. The 3nd Bde/16th IRIA Arm Div would strike eastwards from the narrow Hoveyzeh Salient with two Chieftain MBT battalions and a BMP-equipped mechanized battalion, followed by 2nd Bde with one Chieftain and two BTR-50/60 mechanized battalions. They would drive along the south bank of the Karkheh Kur and roll up the defences, while 1st Bde/16th Div, organized like 2nd Bde, together with elements of the 21st IRIA Inf Div, would pin down the defenders from the north by attacking across the dry 'land bridge', south-west of the village of Tarrah.

This would distract the enemy while Operation Nasr was launched south of Ahvaz. Here, a task force based upon 2nd Bde/92nd IRIA Arm Div would cross the Karun and penetrate the inundations from the east to take the eastern anchor of the Iraqi defences at Dub-e Said. The two arms would then combine and drive down the Ahvaz-Khorramshahr highway while a third offensive, Operation Tavakkol (Trust in God, also written Tavakole), would strike the enemy bridgehead across the Karun north of Abadan with elements of 77th IRIA Inf Div supported by 37th IRIA Arm Bde, to pave the way for the relief of Abadan. The operations around Ahvaz involved some 200 MBTs, and to support Hoveyzeh/Tavakkol there were six self-propelled artillery battalions (M 109 and one with M 107) and a MLRS battery, while to support Nasr there were three battalions of M 109 and three towed batteries, a total of some 155 guns.[2] However, air support was confined to 16 Cobra gunships and four under-strength squadrons of Tigers and Phantoms, some manned by pilots who had only recently been released from prison.[3]

The Iraqi defences exploited the swamps west of Ahvaz, which were some 20km long and 10km wide, to lap against both sides of the Ahvaz-Khorramshahr highway, augmented by anti-tank ditches across the 'land bridge'. Covering the northern defences was the 9th Arm Div (Talia Al-Duri), which held a 40km line mostly shielded by the Karkheh Kur from Hoveyzeh through Achmedabad (the centre of the Iraqi line) to Dub-e Said, where the line ran south along the highway. Duri's 35th Arm Bde invested Susangerd in the west, and (west to east) he had 43rd Arm and 14th Mech Bdes, the latter in the tip of the salient, augmented by battalions of 31st SF Bde, while on his right was 3rd Arm Div's 15th Mech Bde, a force whose total strength was estimated by US intelligence at 556 tanks and 141 guns.[4] With III Corps' 3rd Arm Div and 5th Mech Div fully committed south of Ahvaz, although the arrival of 11th Inf Div was easing their burden, Ni'ami's only tactical/operational level reserve was Colonel Mahmood Shukur Shaheen's 10th Arm Bde, which was on his extreme left flank at Fakkeh, some 80km north of Hoveyzeh, but Baghdad had not anticipated enemy action until March, when the ground had dried.

It was forewarned by COMINT, which, with Soviet technical assistance, exploited poor Iranian communications discipline. Scouting parties, and possibly spies, may have added some details, and Duri had sufficient warning to evacuate his outposts before the blow fell. The IRIA also had a COMINT service under Military Intelligence, the IRIA Sigint Services Communications (ISSC) network, which was based in Tehran, with most sites in south-west Iran monitoring battlefield communications. But all intercepted signals were forwarded to Tehran, although during intense ground fighting the interceptors provide direct support to front-line units.[5]

OPERATIONS HOWEIZEH, NASSR AND TAWAKKOL

The Iranians knew their enemies fought poorly at night and decided to exploit this with probing attacks before dawn on 5 January to discover weaknesses in the enemy line. It was raining on 3 January and foggy the following day, but from 5 January onwards the rains ceased for four days, although the muddy ground meant the 16th IRIA Div spearhead could deploy its MBT battalions only on a narrow front. Deployment was further hampered because the ground between the Karkheh in the north and the Karkheh Kur in the south was criss-crossed with irrigation channels. The Iranians threw bridges across the Karkheh to ensure supplies for their armoured spearhead and the 21st Div's attack.

Despite the advanced warning, the incompetent Talia Al-Duri bungled the defence, allowing the Iranian armoured brigade to drive out of Hoveyzeh while the northern attack penetrated his MLR to take Achmedabad, driving back 43rd Arm Bde, overrunning 9th Arm Div's gun line and threatening the whole Karkheh Kur line. Ni'ami's scout helicopters monitored the advance as he sent up a tank battalion each of 12th Arm Bde/3rd Arm Div and 30th Arm Bde/6th Arm Div to buttress the line, but to stabilize the front he needed Shukur. During the afternoon, he despatched tank transporters for two tank battalions and ordered Shukur to Susangerd (or Khafajiyah as the Iraqis called it), while the mechanized battalion would travel on its tracks, although it did not arrive until 7 January.[6] The corps chief of staff briefed Shukur and ordered him to restore the 43rd Arm Bde front, and as there were only sufficient tank transporters for half of 10th Bde's tanks, he reinforced him with a battalion of T-55s, the reinforced brigade assembling between Susangerd and Hoveyzeh about dawn of 6 January. Meanwhile, Iraqi fighters dispersed Iranian helicopter gunships as the IRIAF made the mistake of using its limited resources for battlefield interdiction rather than close air support, which weakened air support for the Iranian advance.[7]

As Shukur deployed on 6 January, the Iranians continued to exploit their success by building a bridge near Achmedabad and committing a new tank battalion, although this too could advance only along a narrow front. Talia Al-Duri's command post was threatened and he ordered a withdrawal into the second position, but his incompetent handling of the situation caused chaos. By contrast, Ni'ami reacted promptly, aided by the ever-reliable COMINT service, to exploit the road systems on each side of the breakthrough to bring up reserves. Talia Al-Duri's 43rd Arm Bde deployed a tank battalion to block the enemy advance, while 14th Mech Bde's tanks enfiladed the enemy armour from the reserve position as 31st SF Bde was brought in to stiffen the defences. The IrAF was extremely active and largely neutralized enemy artillery fire as well as disrupting gunship support for the Chieftains.

During the day, the 12th Arm Bde's tank battalion came up from the south to support 14th Bde and helped to contain the threat from Achmedabad. In the west, Shukur began his counter-attack from south-west of Susangerd, punching eastward through the Hoveyzeh Salient to secure the dry ground between the Karkheh and the flooded areas to the south. He then planned to strike south to Hoveyzeh, cross the Karkheh Kur and retake 43rd Arm Bde's positions. He had only 80 MBT and deployed them in a single wave at 100-metre intervals between vehicles, with orders to drive at top cross-country speed of 20km/h, firing rapidly at three rds/min when engaging the enemy.[8] An Iranian intelligence officer warned the Ahvaz headquarters the Iraqis might be luring 16th Div into a deadly trap, but his superiors believed they faced only screening forces, a view encouraged by Iraqi tactical withdrawals. During the day, the trap was finally sprung as Shukur pushed from the west, while T-55s and T-62s struck from the south, in a close-range battle which trapped the Iranians against the flooded zone.

The Iranians tried to deploy off the road, but their heavy (55 tonnes) Chieftain tanks often became stuck in the mud, unlike the lighter (3640 tonne) enemy tanks. However, the Chieftain's marksmanship was better and they had superior fire control, based upon the Marconi FV/GCE Mk 4 fire control system, which used a ranging machine gun and Barr and Stroud LF2 laser rangefinder ,while the T-54 and T-62 had only optical sights. The Iranian tanks also had the 120mm

L11A5 gun (range 3km with APDS and 8km with HESH), which could fire a sustained rate of six rounds a minute compared with four to five in the T-54/55, whose 100mm D-10T gun fired BK-17 AP and HEAT rounds with a range of up to a kilometre.[9] But the T-72s were a match for the Chieftains, aided by their TPD-K1 laser rangefinder and 2A46 125mm L/48 smoothbore gun with its APFSDS rounds, which, US intelligence concluded, could out-range by up to a kilometre the rifled guns of the Iranian tanks, while the front glacis armour of the T-72 was virtually impervious to anti-armour fire.[10] By the afternoon, Shukur had secured a bridgehead south of the Karkheh, but was low on ammunition as the Iranians fled the Hoveyzeh Salient, running the gauntlet of Iraqi MBTs and IRIAF friendly fire, which led local commanders to shoot on any aircraft they saw. Among those who reportedly suffered was a Pasdaran company, which included 70 of the 'students' who had seized the American Embassy in Tehran.[11]

The isolation of Hoveyzeh and the Iranian 3rd Bde left the latter running short of fuel and ammunition. In a desperate attempt to relieve them, 16th Div used 2nd Bde to strike from the north with gunship support on 7 January, but the ground here also bogged down vehicles. At the same time, the ZSU-57-2 self-propelled air defence guns inhibited Iranian helicopter operations and allowed the Iraqi gunships to intervene, while the IrAF was also extremely active, using large numbers of cluster bombs. Both sides became intertwined as the IrAF struck targets both on the battlefield and the bridges across the Karkheh and Karkheh Kur around the Hoveyzeh Salient, the Iranians reportedly losing half their vehicles. This air support played a major role in Shukur's survival, for he spent most of the day replenishing fuel and ammunition as well as bringing up the rest of the brigade.

On 8 January, Shukur pushed south to Hoveyzeh and then along the Karkheh Kur to restore the line and recapture 9th Arm Div's lost guns. For their part, the Iranians abandoned the relief operation the following day as the survivors of 3rd Bde picked their way through the flooded zones to safety, having abandoned their vehicles. The Iraqis claimed to have captured some 120 tanks and 65 AFVs, some allegedly with their engines still running, and to have destroyed another 114, while foreign journalists observed about 140 AFVs in the mud.[12]

The biggest single tank action of the Iran-Iraq War involved 450 MBTs from eight Iraqi and three Iranian tank battalions. It is estimated Iraqi losses were between 80 and 130 AFVs, including 60100 MBTs, although Shukur's brigade lost only three T-72s, all to Iranian Cobra gunships with TOW heavy anti-armour missiles, which proved a potent combination during the battle and would continue to do so in the coming months. However, the Cobras lost half their strength, mostly to ground fire.[13] Shukur's brigade was given the credit for the success and was named 'al Qa'qaa' after al Qa'qaa ibn Amr at-Tamimi, who played a key role in the Arab victory over the Persians at Qadisiyya. Colonel Shukur was promoted to brigadier general on 15 May to command 6th Arm Di, and from August 1983 he headed GMID but was dismissed in 1986 following the loss of the Faw Peninsula, which was partly blamed upon poor intelligence, but he would later become 1st Special Corps' chief of staff.[14]

Ni'ami appears to have probed around Susangerd shortly afterwards, but the defenders (reinforced by part of 55th IRIA Air Bde brought in by helicopter) were supported by the remnants of 16th Div. The Iraqi probes were largely based upon artillery bombardments, and were abandoned having achieved little while suffering heavy losses from AGM-65A Maverick guided air-to-surface missiles launched by IRIAF Phantoms.[15]

Meanwhile, the other element of the Iranian offensive, Operation Nasr, was also launched on 5 January, using the 2nd Bde/92nd IRIA Arm Div reinforced by an M47 tank battalion of 77th IRIA Div and a mixture of a Pasdaran battalion and guerrilla force under Dr Mustafa Ali Chamran. A Pasdaran battalion crossed the inundations some 15km south-west of Ahvaz and struck positions around Dub-e Said, but was thrown back by a counter-attack within three days.

Despite these failures, two days after this defeat, and a day after the IRIA abandoned its meagre gains from Hoveyzeh, the IRIA launched the forlorn hope which was Operation Tavakkol. The Iraqi 3rd Arm Div headquarters (Jabar al-Duri) had 6th Arm Bde, whose organic units were augmented battalions of 3rd and 44th Inf Bdes and 26th Arm Bde. On the far side of the Karun, 5th Mech Div had 20th Mech Bde to bolster the salient's northern shoulder, while 49th Inf Bde/11th Div was at Khorramshahr.

The plan called for the 37th IRIA Arm Bde, reinforced by a tank battalion of 77th Div and a Pasdaran battalion, to strike down the Bandar-e-Khomeini highway while 2nd Bde/77th IRIA Inf Div broke out of the Abadan bridgehead up the highway. They were to link, then strike northwards to clear the bridgehead, and there were even dreams of crossing the Karun and retaking Khorramshahr. With only nine combat (armour and infantry) battalions against 17 defending battalions, there was never any prospect of success and the attackers were mowed down, the only consolation being that the IRIA did receive a more realistic understanding of Iraqi defences.[16]

Driven by political rather than military considerations, Bani-Sadr's plan was too ambitious and launched at the wrong time of the year. The IRIA performed poorly, with notable failures in tactical intelligence as well as command and control which slowed its reaction, while there was an over-reliance, like the Iraqis four months earlier, upon armour. The Iraqi performance was uneven, still over-reliant upon armour and short of infantry, yet Saddam was encouraged and believed the victory showed the enemy they could not defeat the Iraqi Army.

The offensive seriously eroded IRIA armoured strength and prestige, while making Ban-Sadr's fall from grace inevitable, and on 11 March, the parliament restricted his powers. The clerics also persuaded Khomeini the IRIA lacked the political commitment to prosecute the war successfully. As a man who had spent his life surrounded by spiritual texts, Khomeini was naturally attracted to the idea of belief overcoming physical obstacles, and increasingly he supported the Pasdaran as the key to military success. IRIA strength would continue to rise during the year and would reach 170,000, while the Pasdaran expanded to at least 50,000, increasingly organized into battalions which could be augmented by the Basiji, who were placed under Pasdaran command on New Year's Day 1981.[17]

Yet the Iranians benefitted from a serious Iraqi security breach when Saddam's press secretary accidentally revealed the Iraqis were intercepting enemy communications. The Iraqis quickly acquired Crypto C-52 mechanical enciphering machines and tried to impose better communications discipline upon the IRIA, and these moves provided a degree of security for the remainder of the year.[18]

The Gathering Storm

As temperature rose from 20°C to 30°C and the ground dried, Susangerd now became the focus for both sides. On 19 March, 35th Arm Bde attacked the town with strong artillery support but made little progress, and the following day, with casualties mounting, Saddam closed down this operation. It was an ominous failure, for the

5: THE IRANIANS STRIKE BACK

IRIAA troops celebrating their initial success during Operation Nassr also known as Operation Hoveyzeh in the West. However, an Iraqi counter-attack was soon to drive them back with heavy losses. (Albert Grandolini Collection)

Iraqis had been unable to take their objectives while the Iranians had demonstrated defensive skill.[19]

The Iraqi failure reinforced Iranian determination to remove the threat to Susangerd. They targeted the Allah Akbar Heights, low dunes (4244 metres) some 25km north-west of Susangerd between the town and the main dune region, which was both the enemy's northern anchor and a base for Gainful missile batteries, which were a constant threat to the IRIAF. Operation Imam Ali was to eliminate the threat, and the task was assigned to of the 8th Najaf-Ashraf Pasdaran Bde, supported by two battalions of 3rd Bde/92nd IRIA Arm Div; the M-60-equipped 231st Tank and BMP-equipped 145th Mech.[20] The attack, launched during the night of 21/22 May, was a simple frontal assault, but the Iraqi defenders were a tank battalion of 35th Arm Bde, a unit totally unsuitable for holding ground, who were rapidly overwhelmed, losing 30 tanks, and it was claimed only nine soldiers returned to claim they never saw their officers.[21]

A counter-attack was launched the following day, but the Pasder stood their ground and beat them off with the aid of M47 Dragon and TOW anti-armour missiles transferred from IRIA supply depots. Nine IRIA self-propelled artillery batteries, mostly M109 but two with M107, now began to pound the Iraqi positions. To prevent an armoured riposte, the Iranians again flooded the low ground around Susangerd, while Pasdaran forces infiltrated across the Karkheh Kur to harass enemy positions and communications. This pressure eventually forced a further Iraqi retreat westwards of 58km on 26 May, nearer the supply base of Bostan.

This minor victory demonstrated to the Pasdaran and their supporters what it could achieve with IRIA support. But there would be a tragic post-script, for on 2 June the new Iranian regime's first Defence Minister, the US-educated scientist turned guerrilla leader Mostafa Ali Chamran, was killed. He was the Pasdaran's first commander in April 1979 before becoming Defence Minister five months later. He always led from the front and his death was reported as due either to a sniper or a mortar bomb. He was succeeded as Pasdaran commander by their intelligence chief, Mohzen Rezai (or Resai), who would hold this position until 1997, although on poor terms with Pasdaran Minister Mohsen Rafiq-Dust. Rezai's father supported Khomeini and was jailed, which led to Rezai Junior being dismissed from military school to become a revolutionary. He would repeatedly fail in his attempts to

A crew member of an Iranian Chieftain during a morning prayer: the vehicle is dug in behind an earthen berm, with the rest of the crew on watch. Chieftains played a prominent role in Operation Hoveyzeh, but suffered heavy losses especially to Malyutka ATGMs and APFSDS shot from Iraqi T-72s. Tankers of the 10th Armoured Brigade were specially advised by their Soviet instructors to use that type of ammunition against Iranian tanks. (Albert Grandolini Collection)

Crew of the 10th Armoured Brigade with one of their tanks in early 1981. The T-72 type was cleared for export only in 1978, and due to Moscow's disagreement with the Iraqi invasion of Iran, no further vehicles of this type were sold to Iraq until July 1982. Nevertheless, the Soviets continued providing spares and ammunition for the type, and their instructors remained in Iraq. Indeed, according to Iraqi reports, they played an important advisory role during Operation Hoveyzeh. (Albert Grandolini Collection)

command all of Iran's ground forces.[22]

To follow on the success, there was a new attack on the Karun bridgehead, Operation Farmande Kole Ghova, Khomeni Rooh Khoda (Khomeini is our Supreme Commander), involving the Najaf-Ashraf Bde augmented by Basij, part of 55th IRIA Air Bde, a tank battalion of

77th IRIA Div and Cobra gunships. The attack began on 11 June and aimed to take the northernmost pontoon bridge at Mared, and while this was not achieved, the defenders, 6th Arm Bde/3rd Arm Div, whose right was close to Salmanieh, were driven back some 5km, which brought the bridge within easy artillery range. It was no longer tenable and was dismantled shortly afterwards, although in revenge the Iraqis increased pressure upon Abadan, now defended by 10,000-15,000 men, including 2nd Bde/77th IRIA Inf Div, with some 60 M47 MBTs.

As the offensive was launched, Khomeini dismissed Bani-Sadr as Commander-in-Chief and replaced him with Fallahi. Then, on 20 June, parliament impeached Bani-Sadr for incompetence and ordered his arrest, although it was not until 24 July that his successor, the radical cleric Mohammad Ali Rajai, was appointed. Bani-Sadr went into hiding, then escaped to France in a defecting IRIAF KC-707 tanker, but the departure of someone whom the clerics regarded as a champion of the Old Guard marked a watershed in IRIA-Pasdaran relations. The clerics could now begin to appreciate the IRIA's sacrifices, which set the stage for better co-operation between the two as they recognized, despite mutual suspicions, they had no option except working together.[23]

It was helped by the fact the IRIA was gaining a new generation of junior leaders who were more in tune with the regime and who had fought alongside the Pasders against the Kurds, yet the clerics continued to restrict the authority of senior officers 'to reduce abuse of power and corruption'.[24] Khomeini waited until 2 September before appointing Colonel (then Brigadier General) Sayad Musa Namjoo as Defence Minister for his work developing IRIA-Pasdaran co-operation. Pasdaran Deputy Commander Ali Yousef Kolahduz was to command the frontline Pasdaran, while IRIAF commander Colonel Javad Fakuri authorized additional close air support for the ground forces.

Khomeini also continued to condemn both the friction between the regular armed forces and the Pasdaran, and also the commissars, noting: "Experts should be allowed to perform their tasks unencumbered by meddling from those who have no knowledge of the subject." Yet the clerical commissars continued to roam formations, headquarters and bases, seeking out those who held 'incorrect' political or religious views, despite Shirazi and Resai's attempts to clip their wings. This was another hurdle facing Iranian offensive plans, already hamstrung by factors including a shortage of qualified staff officers, as well as continued maintenance and logistical problems.[25]

Another reason why the Pasdaran suspicions of the IRIA were eroded was the militia's growing military professionalism created by the harsh realities of war, although ranks would not be introduced until May 1990.[26] Until the summer of 1981, many Pasder were sent to the front without training; indeed early in the year, SFOH had to organize a three-day training course for newly arrived militia.[27] By the summer, the Pasdaran had begun organizing their own military training centres as the 20-30-man platoons, with which they started the war, were expanded into rifle companies with three platoons, while three companies and a heavy weapons company were combined into battalions of some 300-325 men. The battalions were increasingly combined into brigades of three or four battalions, many of which would soon be expanded into divisions of 4,000-4,500 men.[28] Officially, this process began February 1982 with the creation of 27th Mohamad Rasoolallah Bde, which became a division in September 1982, but many Pasdaran regions demonstrated their autonomy by redesignating their formations unofficially before this, from June 1981 in the case of brigades, and by late 1981 with divisions. While the Pasdaran Ministry disapproved, domestic politics forced them to accept the *fait accompli*, then officially roll out the upgrading process.

On 26 July, the Pasdaran, supported by two IRIA tank battalions, tried to regain Hoveyzeh, but this attack ended in disaster. The Iraqi 14th Mech Bde first withdrew under pressure, but three days later staged a successful counter-attack which drove back the Pasders. Undaunted, the Iranians immediately struck west of Susangerd, using elements of 16th and 92nd IRIA Arm Divs, together with Pasdaran/Basij forces, to gain some ground and allow their combat engineers to spend most of the month examining the enemy defences in the region.[29]

By now both sides were exhausted, and during the heat of August they licked their wounds, restricting themselves to bombardments and raids designed to take key terrain as jump-off points for major offensives. Ominously, the Iranians, on 12 August, accused the enemy of using poison gas, which may have been true on a small scale. For their part, the Iranians began to reinforce their fronts significantly by doubling the size of their forces, while the Iraqis built fortifications and sometimes levelled villages to provide fields of fire.[30]

Iranian planning during the summer was hindered by a ferocious terrorist campaign by the People's Mujahideen (or Mojahedin) which killed many leading members of the government and parliament, including Beheshti on 28 June, while the bombing of the SDC on 30 August killed President Rajai. Yet Khomeini continued to demand an operation to end the siege of Abadan, and this would reflect the improved relations between the IRIA and Pasdaran.

Both recognized that the Iraqi superiority in mechanized warfare could be overcome only by exploiting Iranian superiority in manpower and artillery. The architect of the new strategy was the new Chief of the Joint Staff, Major General Qasem Ali Zahirnejhad, who sought to combine the primal force of the Pasdaran with the IRIA's technical expertise, although this was undermined by the shortage of armour, helicopters and artillery ammunition. The SFOH at Ahvaz retained responsibility for operational level planning but no longer had a monopoly on tactical level operations, which would be co-ordinated by *ad hoc* tactical headquarters. There would now be infantry assaults spearheaded by the Pasdaran, which would exploit terrain and be supported by the IRIA with artillery and engineers.

The key was reconnaissance, where both the Pasdaran and IRIA Special Forces would infiltrate enemy positions to conduct covert scouting. This allowed the Iranians to detect weak points and plan to exploit those weaknesses. Diversions, probes and artillery bombardments would pin down the better Iraqi units, while massed infantry assaults with artillery and armoured support would isolate the weak points, which would be stormed at leisure, while the gaps created would be exploited by Pasdaran infantry and IRIA mechanized forces.[31]

A US intelligence history noted: "Iraq was fighting a limited war while Iran was fighting a total one, at least within its capabilities."[32] As the storm clouds gathered, Iraq faced the price of failing to assign military objectives in its poorly planned invasion. Iraqi units had been dumped like flotsam by the high tide of invasion on a long, meandering line from which Saddam would accept neither adjustment nor withdrawal. He was convinced that by defending every inch of captured territory and inflicting unacceptable losses, he would force Tehran to the negotiating table. There was no other strategy; Iraq lacked the resources to stage a war-winning offensive, and prestige precluded the abandonment of Iranian territory without compensation.[33]

Years later, General Makki, who was attached to the Iraqi III Corps in 1981 and became its chief of staff later in the year, illustrated the problem. During an inspection of the front in May 1981, he noticed gaps and suggested expanding the minefields, regrouping forces and bringing up reserves. Corps commander Ni'ami and his chief of staff (General Na'ima al-Mihyawi) disagreed, and asked: "Why should we relinquish ground that we have gained through blood?" When Makki pointed out that at staff college the general had advocated defence in depth, he was told: "Not only do I not agree, the chief of staff does not agree, and Saddam does not agree."[34] Ni'ami had, in fact, wished to abandon exposed positions, but when he suggested that Shanshal propose this to Saddam, he was told: "I will not tell him. You tell him, you are the corps commander."[35]

The problem with this strategy was that Iraq faced a demoralizing war of attrition which it ultimately could not win. Artillery bombardments and raids by the increasingly aggressive Iranians inflicted a steady stream of casualties, although, like Petain at Verdun, the Iraqis tried to spread the pain by rotating units after 40-day tours. Unfortunately, this merely added to problems because units neglected front-line maintenance in anticipation that this would be performed in the rear when they were rotated. Many generals interpreted Saddam's demands that casualties be kept to a minimum by strengthening their defences and avoiding any provocative action such as patrolling beyond the minefields. This was welcome to the troops, who were growing more exhausted and demoralized, for, although they were well fed, they faced the strain of constant vigilance both day and night. Little wonder there was a serious desertion problem, with US intelligence calculating that in the 150,000-200,000-man Iraqi Army there were 6,000-8,000 deserters.[36]

The chronic shortage of infantry led to the decision to rename police COIN formations as infantry brigades, while regular and reserve brigades were augmented with support troops who were often from the Popular Army. It was estimated that by early 1982, abut 10 percent of the Popular Army was in the front line, serving three-month front-line tours.[37] It is doubtful whether the Army commanders really welcomed this 'reinforcement', and Saddam would later regret the decision. He would describe the Popular Army as a 'burden to the regular army.'[38] Yet the Iraqi Army was unprepared for static defence. The DIA noted: "Simple procedures, such as co-ordination of unit boundaries and fire co-ordination planning, were apparently beyond the ability of unit commanders." Commanders were often unable to determine the enemy's main axes, which made them reluctant to commit their reserves for fear they would be held responsible for defeat.[39]

Operation Iman Ali had demonstrated the futility of mechanized units in static defence, and as an interim measure Ni'ami augmented them with battalions from 31st and 32nd SF Bdes, which should have been withdrawn for the training they needed to maintain their edge.[40] Ni'ami had received 11th Inf Div, which was partly deployed around the mouth of the Karun and on the Faw Peninsula to invest Abadan, while 3rd Arm Div concentrated upon the Karun bridgehead.

Saddam was certainly warned about the problems by GMID Director General Dhannoun during the first half of 1981. He pointed out the Iraqis were not mounting continuous surveillance and that during bombardments the troops would remain in their dugouts. Units failed to deploy screening forces, while their defences lacked wire and minefields. He warned that the Iranian attrition strategy might be capable of 'limited success', eroding Iraqi strength and boosting Iranian morale.[41] Despite this, on 25 August, Saddam met

An Iraqi T-55 crew preparing for a mission early in the morning. Like Iranians, Iraqis made extensive use of earth berms to improve protection of their equipment and personnel. These were necessary because of the generally featureless and flat desert of western Khuzestan. (Albert Grandolini Collection)

The crew of an Iranian Chieftain monitoring a road in Khuzestan. Gauging by their clearly relaxed posture, no threat was imminent when this photograph was taken. Note the extensive storage of different kit around the rear top of the turret. Chieftains were generally considered as poor tanks by Iranian crews: although they report receiving excellent technical support, the type was underpowered, and not only the engine and transmission, but even the gun stabilisation malfunctioned frequently. (Tom Cooper Collection)

Wreckage of an IrAAC Mi-8 helicopter being inspected by Iranian troops. Iranian and Iraqi helicopters saw intensive deployment during Operation Hoveyzeh, and each side lost about half-a-dozen of different models at least four of these in air combats or to enemy interceptors. (Albert Grandolini Collection)

Early in 1981, Iraqi Mi-25 helicopter gunships saw their first deployment in larger numbers over a relatively limited sector of the front lines. They deployed about 50 3M11 Falanga (AT-2 Swatter) anti-tank missiles with some success, but primarily used unguided 68mm rockets. At least one was shot down in an air combat with Iranian interceptors. (Tom Cooper Collection)

the General Command of the Armed Forces and laid out his two-pronged strategy, which was to bleed to death the Iranian Army on the battlefield and their economy through attacks on their oil industry and electricity generation facilities.[42]

OPERATION SAMENE-AL-AEME

To meet Khomeini's demand for the relief of Abadan, the Iranians began to plan Operation Samene-al-Aeme from late August, and planning intensified from then although D-Day was not set until 24 September.[43] The immediate objective was to destroy the Karun bridgehead and relieve Abadan, but it was regarded as the first step in the strategy to liberate all of Khuzestan.

Logistics were a major problem because supplies could come only along the highways to Abadan from Ahvaz and Bandar-e-Khomeini, the former within range of long-range Iraqi artillery, while the latter's maritime approaches were interdicted by the IrAF and Iraqi Navy. Fortunately for the Iranians, personnel could be fed in through an airbridge to major cities using Boeing 707, Boeing 747, C-130 Hercules and F.27 Troopship transports.[44] In addition, 77th IRIA Div engineers built a road, the Unity Road, into the town from the east, while other engineers built a 60km canal from the Karun River to prevent the enemy flooding the battlefield.[45]

The Iranians aimed to squeeze out the salient, but first there would be a diversion in the north to draw off reserves. Supported by elements of 16th IRIA Arm Div and 55th IRIA Air Bde, plus nine batteries (54 guns, including 18 towed tubes), some 3,000-4,000 Pasdaran struck on the night of ½ September, and for three weeks mixed company-sized units conducted a hit-and-run campaign along the northern face of the Ahvaz Salient against 9th Arm Div (14th Mech and 43rd Arm Bdes). Many broke through the berms, and the attacks intensified from 18 September as Ni'ami weakened the defences of Abadan by moving 6th Arm Bde/3rd Arm Div northwards to contain the threat, upon which the Iraqis claimed to have inflicted 7,700 casualties, although they hinted their own casualties were similar. The IRIAF was extremely active in this diversion, and from 21 August to mid-September dropped nearly 170 tonnes of bombs.

Meanwhile, some 20,000 men were assembled for the main offensive, supported by another 15,000 in Abadan. The operation was directed by the 77th IRIA Inf Div's commander, Colonel Shahab-Al-Din Javadi, who set up his headquarters at Bander-e Mashur, and its main axes were predictably along the two highways into Abadan. The northern axis (along the Ahvaz highway) had Javadi's 3rd Bde and the southern axis 37th IRIA Arm Bde (three armoured and mechanized battalions), while Javadi's remaining brigades faced the southern (1st Bde) and eastern (2nd Bde, with a mechanized battalion) faces of the salient. Dispersed among the IRIA were some 8,000 Pasdaran of the 8th Najaf-Ashraf and 14th Imam Hossein Bdes, reinforced by Basij, and the offensive would be supported by six self-propelled (M 109) and five towed batteries. Heavy weapons were at a premium, and US intelligence calculated the Iranians had in the area only 66 tanks and 67 guns, with 64 APC.

The Iraqi bridgehead was some 20km long and 15km deep between a dry flood plain south of Mared, the River Bahmanshir and the Musa Marshes. It was supplied by two PMP bridges at Qasabeh and Hafar on the western bank of the Karun, covered by scattered tank and mechanized platoons of 12th Arm Bde augmented by Popular Army units and 31st SF Bde. The 7,000-man garrison, which was supported by 11 batteries augmented by a dozen on the opposite bank of the Shatt, consisted in the north of 8th Mech Bde, reinforced by two battalions of the 31st SF Bde and Popular Army units, and in the south by 44th Inf Bde, mostly distributed in company or platoon strongpoints. Having lost 6th Arm Bde, 3rd Arm Div was reduced to two brigades, but was joined near the mouth of the Karun by 44th and 49th Inf Bdes/11th Inf Div.

Ni'ami had retained 10th Arm Bde as his tactical/operational level reserve, but the Iraqis were anxious to conserve their precious T-72s and operated them with T-55/62 tank units, which acted as 'missile catchers'.[46] The brigade was near Basra and the Iraqis clearly received some warning of the wrath to come, because Shukur began to move part of his brigade eastwards. Its presence would help to give the Iraqis, according to US intelligence, 300 tanks and 62 guns, with 175 ICV/APC, and they had strong air defences, including seven batteries of Gainful. The Iranians were fully informed about the state of the enemy defences because the Iraqis had not cleared civilians from the villages and also failed to conduct patrols.

On the night of 26/27 September, small teams of Pasdaran troops and IRIA commandos struck along the whole length of the Karun bridgehead, often infiltrating along company and battalion boundaries. They isolated some positions, which the Pasdaran units would then storm from all sides to overwhelm the defenders, tactics especially successful against Popular Army troops. Even if they were unable to storm the positions, the Iranians inflicted heavy casualties to bewilder the defenders and panic all levels, including the higher echelons.

As dawn broke, the Iranians launched conventional attacks, with strong fixed- and rotary-wing air support, down the highways from Darkhovin in the north and Bandar-e Mashur in the east, the latter including a subsidiary thrust along the soft-topped embanked road from the highway to Mared as temperatures rose to around 40°C. Iranian tactics emphasized massed infantry attack, often behind a rolling artillery barrage and with tank support, but this was limited in distance and the infantry tended to move in 'bounds' of up to 3km.[47] Inflexible fire control arrangements meant the Iraqi artillery appears to have played little part in the defence.

The Mared defenders were ordered to withdraw to avoid encirclement, but no preparations were made.[48] As news of this withdrawal flashed along the line, it caused panic, especially among Popular Army units, and during the morning men began to stream westward towards the two bridges, which were now under air attack. As the northern defences collapsed, those in the south also came under pressure and a further withdrawal began here. At this point, IRIAF attacks cut both the Qasabeh and Hafar bridges, and increasingly panicky men desperately sought to escape the oncoming Iranians; some seized small boats or built makeshift rafts to cross the Karun to safety. Meanwhile, with little opposition, the Iranian tide lapped ever closer to the Karun.

To stabilize the situation, 10th Arm Bde was committed but confined itself to firing across the Karun, enfilading the Iranian advance to cover the eastern approaches to the bridge, which engineers prepared to demolish. It lost some AFVs to the deadly Cobra/TOW combination, but the Iranians would lose nine gunships in this operation.[49]

Ni'ami's efforts, and those of the gunners, gave the Iraqis time to evacuate possibly half of their troops, but little equipment, before the bridge was blown up on 28 September, leaving them with only an enclave in southern Khorramshahr. The Iranians mopped up and completed the relief of Abadan the following day, and their success compelled a major reorganization of the Iraqi III Corps' forces to face

The crew of this T-72 from the 10th Armoured Brigade monitor helicopter activity over the front line ahead of them. Their tank was well dug in behind a berm but its 2A46 main gun could be depressed by only six degrees, which meant that in the event of a major battle, the vehicle usually had to leave the safety of its 'fox hole'. (Albert Grandolini Collection)

the potential new threat from the east: 9th Arm Div was transferred from the northern face of the Ahvaz Salient to the Karun front north of 3rd Arm Div, and its sector was taken over by 6th Arm Div.

The Iranians had achieved a spectacular victory, which removed a major incursion, but their claims of capturing 200 AFVs, including 40100 tanks, and to have inflicted 34,000 casualties (more than eight times the strength of the bridgehead garrison), were grossly exaggerated. US intelligence put the number of captured AFVs at 3040 (based upon satellite images) and the total casualties of both sides at 5,000. It seems the Iraqis suffered some 1,800 casualties and lost 1,500 prisoners, a high proportion from the Popular Army, and 300 vehicles, as well as five 155mm guns, while the Iranians may have been left with a casualty list twice that of the defenders. The IRIAA also suffered severely, losing 14 helicopters, but IRIAF losses were lighter, and their operations more effective, thanks to the skilled use of aerial reconnaissance. The victory was due to the Iranians successfully harnessing the strengths of the IRIA and Pasdaran into a winning team, as confidence grew that Iraqi positions could not withstand Iranian infantry attack. The joy was mixed with sadness, for the C-130 carrying almost all the recently appointed Iranian military leadership Namjoo, Fallahi, Kolahduz and Fakuri crashed in the Kharizak Mountains some 10km from Tehran on 30 September and all were killed, depriving Iran of an experienced and proven command team.

The new Defence Minister was Major General Mohamad Salimi, who joined the Imperial Iranian Army in 1950 and rose through hard work and dedication. His opposition to the Shah, which led to imprisonment, together with his piety and loyalty to the new regime, made this thoroughly professional soldier acceptable to everyone. On 2 October, Brigadier General Qasem Ali Zahirnejhad replaced Fallahi, while Major General Ali Sayad Shirazi (also written Seyyed-Shirhani) became Commander of IRIA Ground Forces, the latter also known for his piety, which led the Americans to call him 'The Man of God'.[50]

Shirazi shared Khomeini's views on the Islamification of the IRIA, and as liaison officer in Kurdistan with the Pasdaran was dismissed by Bani-Sadr for his support for brutal repression. Clerical influence ensured he was reinstated as 28th Inf Div commander in Kordistan Province and, following Bani-Sadr's dismissal, he became commander of the North West Forward Operations Headquarters

The Iranians lost dozens of armoured vehicles during Operation Nassr/Hoveyzeh, and over 1,000 by 1987. Few were actually destroyed: most were abandoned due to technical failures and collected by the triumphant Iraqis. This collection includes a few M47Ms, M48s and M60s, at least one Chieftain and two Scorpions. (Albert Grandolini Collection)

(NWFOH). Shirazi's background ensured that he and Pasdaran commander Mohsen Rezai developed a good working relationship, the general integrating the Pasdaran with the NWFOH.[51]

The loss of the bridgehead also led to major changes in the Iraqi command. Ni'ami's position had been undermined and he was replaced in III Corps by 5th Mech Div commander General Al-Qadhi, who would need to focus upon keeping the enemy east of the Karun. With II Corps under mounting pressure, communications into northern Khuzestan needed to be secured, and on 22 October IV Corps was established under Major General Hisham Sabah Al-Fakhry to cover this supply route from threats which might emerge from the sand dune region or up the Karkheh valley. The corps was carved from the right of II Corps (1st Mech and 10th Arm Divs), together with the newly formed 14th Inf Div under Brigadier General Suhail Ismael Al-Adhami, a competent but outspoken commander.[52]

Chapter 5 Notes

1. For Hoveyzeh/Nassr, see Buchan, pp.341, 458 f/n 15; Cooper & Bishop, pp.11314, 135 n. 183; Farrokh, pp.35758; Hiro, p. 49; *Lessons*, pp.11214; Malovany, pp.16266; Murray & Woods, pp.14346, 14950; Pollack, *Arabs*, pp.19395; *Saddam's Generals*, pp.13233; O'Ballance,

pp.60–63; Pollack, p.194; Ward, pp.253–54. US AISC pp.4-37, 4-39, 4-43, 4-44, 4-45, Fig. 4-14, 5-9, Figs 5-5, 5-6. This incorrectly identifies the defenders as 6th Arm Div, as does Pollack, but provides much useful information; Imposed War website. I would like to express my gratitude to General Makki for reviewing this chapter and making corrections as well as numerous helpful comments. This and all later accounts also benefit from both sides' communiqués published in the *Baghdad Times* and *Tehran Times* and/or broadcast and published in the BBC's 'Summary of World Broadcasts' or the US FSIB.
2. US AISC, p.4-37.
3. Cooper & Bishop, p.113.
4. US AISC, p.4-37.
5. DIA DDB-1100-343-85, p.42.
6. Shukur had two battalions of T-72s which Iraq received from July 1979. A combination of maintaining Iraqi prestige and a shortage of spares would restrict the battlefield use of the T-72 until 1982. DIA DDB-1100-IZ-81, p.xx, DDB-1100-343-85, p.62. Details of Shukur's counter-attack from General Makki based upon Shukur's memoirs.
7. Cooper & Bishop, p.113.
8. A T-72 carries 39 rounds, while a T-55 has 43. Foss, *Armour and Artillery 2007–2008*, pp.105, 126.
9. For tank gun performance, see Foss, *Armour and Artillery 2000–2001*, pp. 93, 124–25.
10. Foss, *Armour and Artillery 2007–2008*, p.104; US AISC, p.4-43.
11. Cooper & Bishop, p.114.
12. The Iraqis had been interested in Chieftains since September 1976, but the British informed Baghdad their production facilities were fully committed to meeting the Iranian order. By February 1981, the Iraqis had probably captured 100–150 Chieftains, and asked the British to refurbish them. Most were transferred for this to western Iraq near the Jordanian border, with a few being left at Camp Taji, here they were discovered by American forces in 2003, but as the Chieftain needed special ammunition and had a poor automotive system, most of the tanks were given to Jordan. UK NA FCO 8/2793, 2845, 3023, 4164.
13. Cooper & Bishop, p.114; *Lessons*, p.114. US AISC, p.4-44.
14. Information from General Makki.
15. O'Ballance, p.63; Pollack, pp.194–95.
16. Cooper & Bishop, p.114; *Lessons*, p.112; O'Ballance, p.64; Pollack, p.194. Imposed War website.
17. Cooper & Bishop, p.113; Ward, pp.246–47; Samuel, p.3 and p.3 f/n 8. DIA DDB-1100-342-86, p.2.
18. Murray & Woods, pp.70–71; *Saddam's Generals*, pp.20–21. The author would like to thank Mr Ralph Simpson of the Cipher Machines website (ciphermachines.com) and Mr Paul Reuvers of the Crypto Museum for help on cryptographic matters.
19. Farrokh, p.358; Hiro, p.50.
20. For Iman Ali and follow-on operations, see Buchan, p.339; Farrokh, p.358; *Lessons*, p.115; *Saddam's Generals*, pp.120–21. This claims the defenders were 26th Arm Bde, but this was with 5th Mech Div near Abadan. US AISC, pp.5-17, 5-20, Figs 5-8, 5-11.
21. The difficulties of holding ground in tank against infantry combat are illustrated in the 2014 Brad Pitt movie '*Fury*'.
22. DIA DDB-1100-342-86, Appendix B, p.74.
23. Cooper & Bishop, p.126; Farrokh, pp.360–61; *Lessons*, pp. 114, 117–18, 420; O'Ballance, p.65; Ward, pp.254–55.
24. Ward, pp.245, 247.
25. O'Ballance, p.65; Ward, p.255; US AISC, pp.5-15, 5-17. Website AllRefer.com, Country Study and Country Guide, Iran.
26. Davis, p.27.
27. Murray & Woods, p. 81.
28. Based upon CRRC SH-GMID-D-000-529 and DIA DDB-1100-342-86. IRIA companies had about 140–150 men and battalions up to 600.
29. Malovany, pp.168–69; Murray & Woods, p.172.
30. *Lessons*, pp.117, 122; O'Ballance, pp.64–65; Pollack, p.195. US AISC, p.5-2.
31. For the Iranian forces, see Ward, p.253; DIA DDB-1100-342-86, pp.5, 46; DDB-2680-103-88, p.5.
32. US AISC, p.5-33.
33. Op cit, pp.5-1, 5-20.
34. *Saddam's Generals*, p.120.
35. Op cit, pp.120–21, and information from General Makki.
36. US AISC, p.5-34.
37. Hiro, p.89. Hiro estimated Popular Army strength at 500,000, but this is an exaggeration.
38. *Lessons*, p.426; Marashi & Salama, pp.154–55; *Project 1946*, p.59.
39. DIA DDB-1100-343-85, pp.32, 59–60, 66.
40. *Project 1946*, p.69.
41. Murray & Woods, p.149.
42. Op cit, pp.172–73.
43. For Samen-e-al-Aeme, see Cooper & Bishop, p.127; Farrokh, pp. 361–62; Hiro, pp.52–53; **Lessons**, pp.117, 123–24; Malovany, pp.180–81; Murray & Woods, p.173; O'Ballance, pp.66–67; Pelletiere, p. 41; Pollack, pp.195. US AISC, pp.5-9, 5-15, 5-20, 5-29, Figs 5-7, 5-11, 5-12. A.R. Tucker's article 'Armored Warfare in the Gulf and Armies of the Gulf War'. Samen-e-al- Aeme was the Shi'ites' eighth Imam, also written Samen-ol-A'emeh, Samenol A'emeh, Thamil ul' Aimma or Thamen-ol-A'emeh.
44. Cooper-Bishop, p.86.
45. Buchan, p.351; Davis, p.23; A.H. Cordesman, *The Iran-Iraq War and Western Security 1984–1987: Strategic Implications and Policy Options* (London: Jane's, 1987), p.61.
46. DIA DDB-1100-343-85, pp.52, 62.
47. O'Ballance, p.68.
48. It is unclear who made this order, either Ni'ami or Saddam, probably the former. Murray & Woods, p.173.
49. Reports that the brigade lost a third of its tanks are exaggerated, the DIA concluding that from 1981–1985 only 25-50 T-72 were destroyed, mostly by ATGM, and 15–18 captured, of which one was reportedly used as a target during evaluations of the missile. The Russians tested captured TOW, and in October 1981 passed on detailed reports through the Iraqi Military Attaché in Moscow, to GMID. CRRC SH-GMID-D-001-084; DIA DDB-1100-343-85, pp.52, 62.
50. Cooper & Bishop, pp.127–28; *Lessons*, p.125; O'Ballance, p.68. Website AllRefer.com, Country Study and Country Guide, Iran Joint Crisis: Supreme Defense Council of Iran, 1980. Harvard Model United Nations 2012. Copy on website www.harvardmun.org/wp-content/uploads/2012/01/JCCIran1.pdf.
51. Ward, p.255; DIA DDB-1100-342-86, Appendix B, p.72.
52. Based on information from General Makki.

MAPS

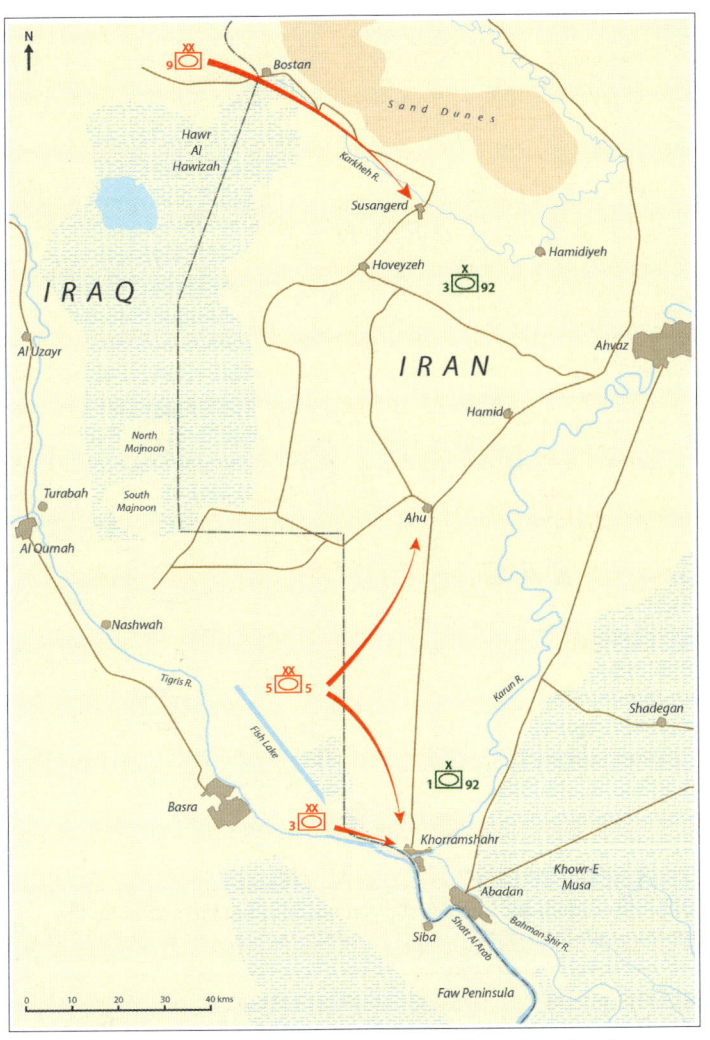

Khuzestan invasion September 1980: The Iraqi invasion aimed to seize western Khuzestan and the north coast of the Shatt.

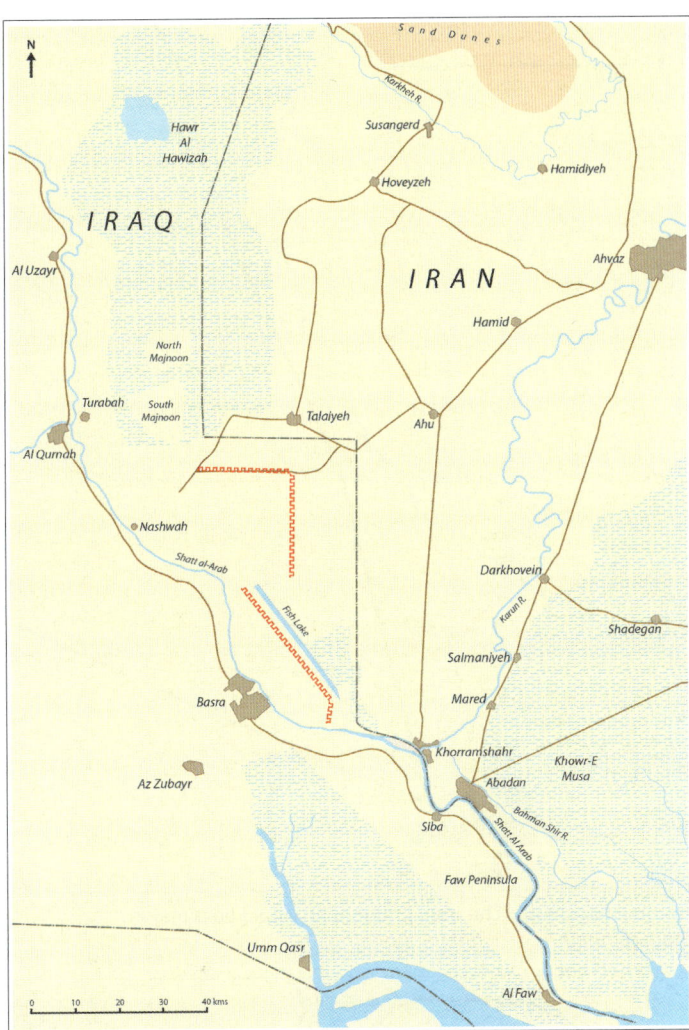

Southern Battlefield: The key features of the southern battlefield.

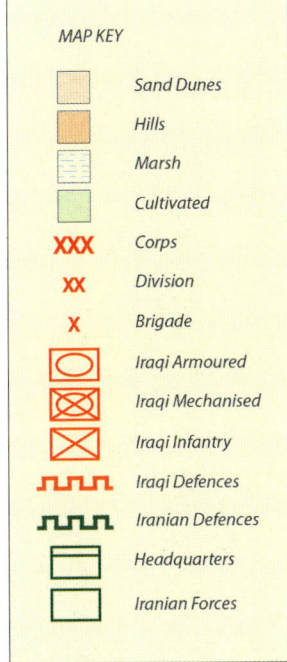

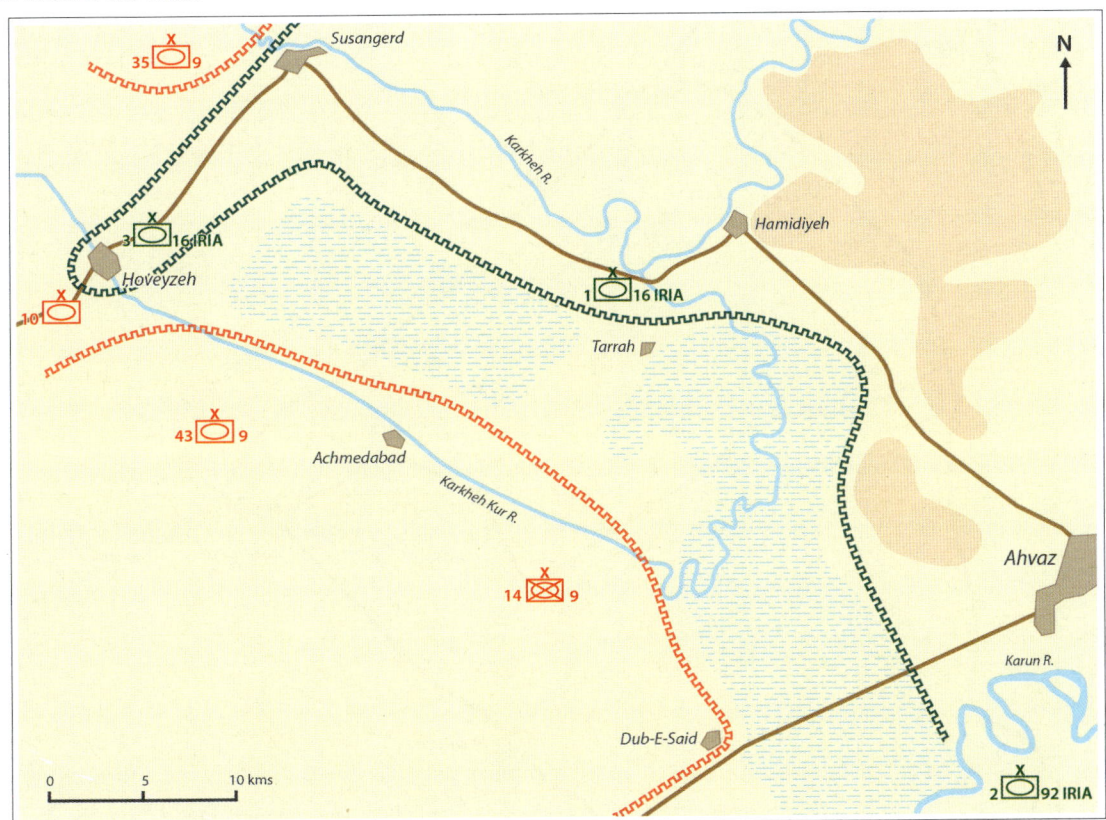

Operations Hoveyzeh/Nassr January 1981: The first Iranian attempt at a counter-offensive which collapsed in failure.

53

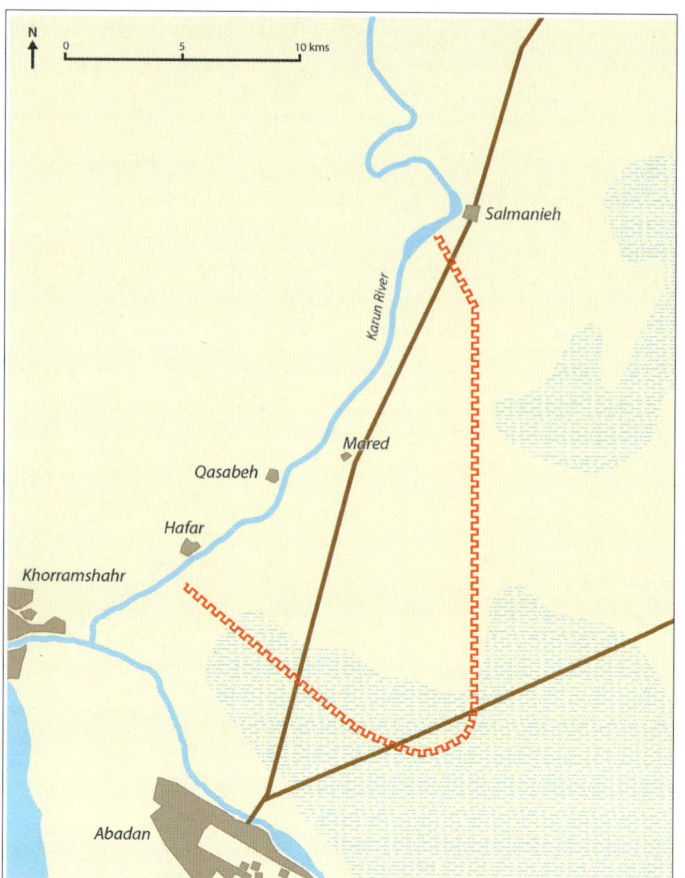

Karun Bridgehead: The Iraqi bridgehead would be a major battleground.

Operation Imam Ali: Iran's first great success set the scene for the recovery of Khuzestan

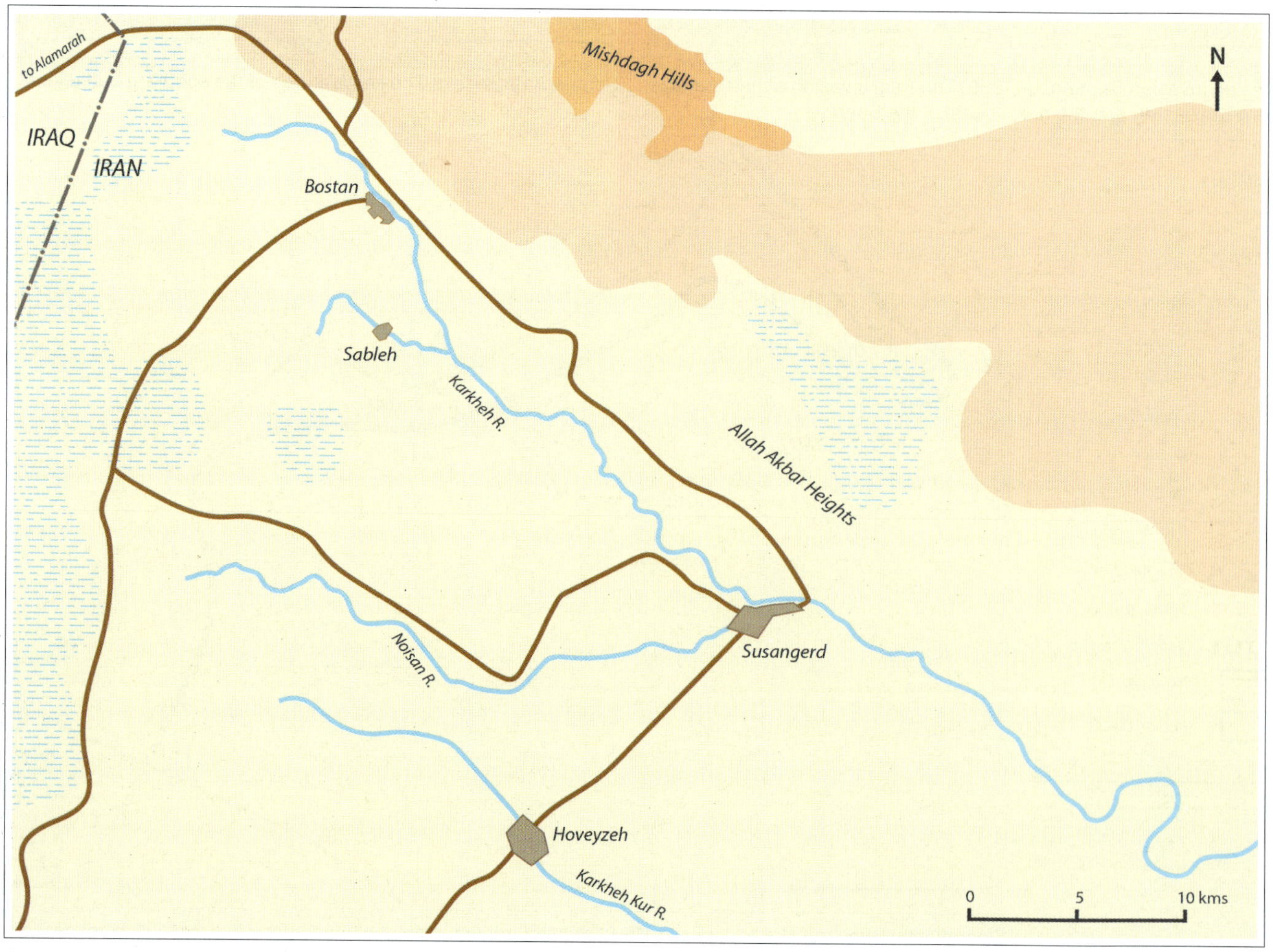

Operation Beit ol Mogaddas: This Iranian offensive was an overwhelming victory over extended Iraqi forces who were routed.

6
The writing on the wall

Replacing the Iranian high command delayed Khomeini's hopes of clearing Khuzestan, but another step to this goal was being prepared during October and November. The Iraqis had two major supply lines into southern Khuzestan, from the south through Salamcheh and Khorramshahr and from the north through Bostan, and they had extended the road network in between.[1]

From the summer, the Iranians had exploited the terrain and gaps in the enemy defences to harass the northern supply routes and tightened their control of the sand dunes north of the Karkheh. To the south, the Iraqi lines followed the Amarah-Ahvaz highway before turning south at the Allah Akbar Heights and running south to Hoveyzeh after crossing the Rivers Sableh, Al Abbas and Noisan (also Neisan or Meysan), which would restrict a counter-attack from the Karkheh defences which were still augmented by inundations.

OPERATION TARIGH AL-QODS, NOVEMBER–DECEMBER 1981

An Iranian planning team led by Colonel Aqbal Mohammad Zadeh, and including Colonels Masood Bakhtiari and Houshang Navabi, began to draft a plan, Tarigh al-Qods (The Way to Jerusalem), to cut the northern supply line during the rainy season by taking Bostan.[2] Not only would this end the threat to Susangerd, but it would also pave the way for destroying the Ahvaz Salient; the Iranians intended to envelop the enemy with a surprise attack from the sand dune region, that was held only by light screening forces, as well as along the south bank of the Karkheh, with the arms linking at Bostan.[3]

A significant feature would reflect the growing professionalism of the Pasdaran. During the second half of 1981, some Pasdaran brigades were expanded into light infantry divisions, usually in three brigades. One was the 14th Imam Hossein Bde, now a division, which used guns captured in the Karun bridgehead to establish its own artillery department, although generally the Pasdaran remained dependent upon the IRIA for armour, artillery and engineering support.

The attackers were organized into two task forces. The northern force, with some 9,000 men, led by the 14th Imam Hossein Pasdaran Div, would sweep through the sand ridge area, and was supported by the 1st Bde/77th IRIA Inf Div (Colonel Aminian) with an M-47 battalion, and a Chieftain battalion of Colonel Bahrami's 3rd Bde/92nd IRIA Arm Div. The southern one, with some 11,500 men, under 31st Ashura Pasdaran Div, would advance along the north bank of the Karkheh and would consist of the division's three brigades, supported by another three Pasdaran brigades, of which the 15th Imam Hassan and 25th Karbala would be on the north bank of the Karkheh, while the 34th Sijjad Bde would be on the southern bank, supported by Colonel Zamanfar's 2nd Bde of 16th IRIA Arm Div with Chieftains. The offensive would be supported by five battalions of 33rd Artillery Group, 57 IRIAF aircraft and the IRIAA, which had received a new shipment of TOW missiles.

Zadeh planned to pin down the defenders in the Karkheh valley by a combination of traditional artillery preparation and Pasdaran assault supported by 16th Arm Div, while Imam Hossein worked its way around the enemy's open northern flank to emerge deep in the rear around Bostan. The latter moved out on the night of 28/29 November, as airborne troops landed by helicopter and took the key

By late 1980, Iranian President Bani Sadr was facing growing opposition from the clerics. He and the military were also under pressure to launch the first offensive against the occupying Iraqis as soon as possible. In an effort to restore his prestige, he authorized Operation Nassr/Hoveyzeh in January 1981. He is shown during one of his many visits to the front line, surrounded by IRIA personnel and a watchful cleric. (Albert Grandolini Collection)

Two Iranian soldiers behind a corner, ready to attack an enemy position inside Susangerd, as soon as their leader has thrown his grenade. (Albert Grandolini Collection)

An Iranian MG1-gunner inside a fortified position in Susangerd. (Albert Grandolini Collection)

Exhausted Iranian Army and Pasdaran troops wandering through Susangerd, after securing it from the Iraqis, in January 1981. (Albert Grandolini Collection)

passes in the Mishdagh or Mushtaq Hills (Kuh-e Mish-Dagh) east of Bostan to ease their advance.

An increase in radio traffic and aerial reconnaissance alerted Iraqi intelligence that something was in the wind, but little more. On 14 November, the GMID concluded that while the enemy would renew their attack at some point, until then they would hold the front with lightly armed troops and recommended limited offensives all along the front to throw the enemy off-balance. Another assessment concluded the destruction of Iranian armour during Operation Hoveyzeh meant the enemy would now rely upon artillery and massed infantry assaults.[4]

The Iraqi line east of Hoveyzeh was held by 5th Mech Div (minus 26th Arm Bde), while the 100km front west of Hoveyzeh to the border was held by 14th Inf Div with four brigades (11,000 men), supported by four artillery battalions (70 guns). The Iraqi formations were, from south to north, 48th Inf and 93rd Res Bdes holding the 55km line from Hoveyzeh to the Karkheh, while north of the river were 31st SF Bde and 26th Arm Bde, neither of which was suitable for holding the 30km stretch of line. In reserve was 14th Div's 422nd Inf Bde.

At 12:30 a.m. on 29 November, SFOH ordered the offensive to begin, but at dawn revolutionary fervour overcame military precision. Anxious to attack the enemy, the Pasdaran ignored the IRIA fire schedule and charged through the rain in the first of what would be quickly dubbed 'human wave' assaults. Most swarmed past the company strongpoints, exploiting ravines to press on to the rear, for, as US intelligence noted: "The Iranians used 'human wave' tactics but carefully orchestrated them against exposed or isolated Iraqi positions."[5] The 93rd Bde bore the brunt of the assault and appears to have disintegrated, and by capturing the bridge over the Sableh at 10:00 a.m. the Pasdaran isolated Bostan from the south.

As the battle raged for the town, Imam Hossein had been steadily advancing through the sand dunes, supported by IRIA armour.[6] During the night of 29/30 November, it began to emerge behind 26th Arm Bde, which fell back in confusion, exposing the rear of the lightly armed 31st SF Bde, which was overwhelmed as the Iranians, making increased use of combined-arms tactics with air support, threatened the 14th Div gun line. IV Corps sent 10th Arm Div's 17th Arm and 24th Mech Bdes, 6th Arm Div's 30th Arm Bde, the new 51st Arm Bde and 422nd Bde, together with a Republican Guard battalion, all under Shukur's command, to stabilize the situation. Initially they covered the 15km Iraqi retreat northwards to a more defendable point on the frontier between the dunes and marshes, which they retained after a bitterly fought night battle.

In the south, during the evening of 30 November, the Pasdaran stormed Bostan (renamed Tarigh al-Qods by the Ayatollah on 6 December), while Sijjad marched westwards towards the Marshes along the minor river valleys which sheltered them from enemy mechanized counter-attacks. The Iraqi 9th Arm Div sent 35th Arm Bde to reinforce the battered 48th Bde, and together they established a new line some 30km south of Bostan. From their new positions, the Iraqis launched counter-attacks which lasted until 6 December and regained 7km to the River Noisan before both sides broke off the battle.

The Iranians claimed to have captured 1,300 troops, together with 100 MBTs, 70 APCs and 19 guns, and while this is an exaggeration, the Iraqis certainly suffered heavy material losses. The 31st SF Bde was destroyed, and probably the 93rd Res Bde, which would suggest some 3,000 casualties, while an Iranian source claims they suffered 6,000 casualties, which, if true, amounted to a third of the attackers.[7] After the attack, a furious Saddam Hussein reportedly dismissed senior officers involved in the defeat and demoted others.[8]

The Pasdaran analyzed their experiences during a January seminar in Tehran and concluded that they should swamp the enemy with infantry while the IRIA provided support and technical services. The Pasdaran now decided upon a major expansion and began to raise at least a brigade in every province of the country. They also demanded tanks and artillery, but the IRIA declined, arguing that there was no time to train the crews.[9]

THE SINEWS OF WAR

At the outbreak of war both sides faced embargoes. Moscow's would have had less effect upon Iraq if Saddam's plans had worked, but the effects increased as the war became protracted. When Saddam revealed his plans on 6 July, he airily dismissed fears that Russia would not replace munitions, especially shells and bombs, yet within a week of the invasion his generals were reporting consumption of 15 percent of the 130mm ammunition consumed, together with

An Iranian infantryman prays in front of his dugout. The Iranians rarely dug deep trenches, and this one barely waist-deep is a good example of their usual practice. (Albert Grandolini Collection)

Operation Tarigh al-Qods (The Path to Jerusalem), in November and December 1981, was one of the first major Iranian successes of the war. It not only regained the town of Bostan, but also a large number of vehicles left behind by the Iraqis. Among these was this BTR-60, possibly knocked out by an RPG operator, like the one in the foreground. (Albert Grandolini Collection)

up to four percent of some tank ammunition.[10] Greece and Turkey offered to provide Saddam with 155mm and 175mm ammunition for captured Iranian guns but too few were captured to make deliveries viable, although Baghdad later diversified its artillery inventory with towed 155mm ordnance from Yugoslavia, which he praised on 22 November 1980 for supplying everything requested.[11] Towards the end of 1980, Greece and India began to supply 130mm and 155mm artillery ammunition under threat of the loss of Iraqi oil.

The spares problem was acute in an AFV fleet dominated by Russian vehicles and the Soviet philosophy shaped to meet the needs of armed forces with few technically-qualified personnel. Spares were replaced after a specific time, rather than when they were failing, as with Western vehicles, so that consumption was high, while Russian spares were not designed for prolonged lives. Soviet vehicles were also designed for cold weather and tended to overheat in the desert, a major problem for troop carriers and the T-72.

Yet Baghdad was not totally dependent upon the Warsaw Pact, and the pre-war diversification programme was accelerated. Brazil received a new $1 billion contract for light armour, including Cascavel, EE-11 Urutu wheeled APC, together with EE-15 4x4, EE-25 and EE-50 6x6 trucks and ammunition. Under a pre-war contract, France would, from 1981, supply 1,000 HOT long-range anti-armour missiles, while Thomson-CSF began to build a radio transceiver factory and won contracts for field telephone equipment.[12] Contracts were also placed with South Korea for commercial soft skin vehicles such as trucks and 4x4 light all-terrain vehicles, while Italy also won a contract for Campagnola Fiat 4x4 light all-terrain vehicles.[13]

Cairo was an enthusiastic supporter of Baghdad, and in March 1981 supplied 4,000 tonnes of materiel, most from army inventories, including T-55s, Walid 4x4 wheeled APCs and artillery. During the war, Egypt was estimated to have supplied $500 million worth of equipment and munitions, although the quality of this aid was uneven. The armour and artillery would have seen extensive service in Egyptian hands and have limited life, while the Walid, which was similar to the BTR-40, was essentially a reconnaissance or counter-insurgency vehicle, but the ammunition would undoubtedly have been valuable. Iraq's other significant Arab friend was Jordan, which ostensibly ordered GHN-45 155mm gun-howitzers from Noricum in Austria and then secretly transferred them across the border into Iraq.

Iran had some friends in the Arab world, notably Syria and Libya, who channeled Soviet origin equipment, spares and ammunition to Tehran, but this would remain a trickle and Iran remained almost as

A dug-in Iraqi T-62. The 2A20 smoothbore gun of this tank could also only be depressed by six degrees, severely restricting its value in defensive battles. (Albert Grandolini Collection)

dependent upon the United States as Iraq was upon the Soviet Union.[14] The confrontation with Washington doomed any chance that the IRIA might regain direct access to US stocks of equipment, spares and ammunition, the Iranians having bitten the hand that fed them. Yet just as Moscow's allies were willing to ignore Soviet embargoes, so were Washington's, who were eager to meet Iranian requirements for oil or cash. Taiwan and South Korea might not be willing to supply equipment,t but they could provide spares; indeed, Iranian F-5 fighter-bombers depended upon these sources. For new equipment, Iran had to turn to the Soviet Union and China, the latter receiving a contract for Type 63 107mm MLRS, while Brazil, a major supplier to Iraq, would deliver light armour and munitions, especially for aircraft, to Iran through Libya.

As a prolonged war became inevitable, from 1981 both sides found it difficult to pay for the growing amounts of equipment and munitions they needed. In the aftermath of the Holy Day War Arab oil blockade, the price of oil more than tripled to around $13 a barrel, with OPEC setting the price and production quotas to fuel a boom for oil producers. But demand then eased as the world used oil more efficiently to force down the price from $36.71 per barrel in 1980 to $31.71 in 1981. A desperate Tehran decided to undercut the OPEC price and almost double production, and by 1982 was selling at $30.20

Iraqi mechanized infantry pose with a large picture of Saddam Hussein, atop a T-55 dug in somewhere along the Karoun River in 1981. (Albert Grandolini Collection)

A T-55 drives through the ruins of Khorramshahr in 1981. Battles there cost the Iraqis heavy casualties, in both men and vehicles. (Albert Grandolini Collection)

A T-62 approaching one of the pontoon bridges across the Karoun. These bridges were vital to support the Iraqi bridgehead investing Abadan. Both came under threat during the summer of 1981, and eventually had to be blown up during Iran's Operation Samene-al-Aeme. (Albert Grandolini Collection)

An Iraqi 180mm S-23 towed gun fires on the Khuzestan front in 1981. This weapon had a range of 30.4km, which was less than the 175mm M107 deployed by the Iranians. The Soviets proved quite reluctant to deliver larger number of S-23s, and Iraq received only one battery of them. (Albert Grandolini Collection)

a barrel and producing 2.3 million barrels a day against the OPEC quota of 1.2 million.[15] Iran had the advantage of unrestricted access to the sea, which eased exports through the Straits of Hormuz. Iraq was dependent upon overland pipelines through Turkey and Syria; the former vulnerable to Kurdish guerrilla attacks and the latter running through the territory of Iraq's arch rival and Tehran's friend.

INTERNATIONAL SUPPORT

By early 1981, Moscow recognized its bid for rapprochement with Tehran had failed and began to mend fences with Baghdad, with arms shipments resuming in May. A new agreement, reportedly worth $1 billion, was signed on 19 September, which included T-72B/G and T-62 MBT, BMD-1 ICVs and artillery, with deliveries accelerated in 1983 and 1984.[16] An order for T-55s was also placed in Moscow, but was sub-contracted to Czechoslovak and Polish factories because Russian production had ceased, and they also provided some T-72s and BMP-1.

French arms exports to Iraq increased. During 1981, GIAT won a $600 million contract for Giat Grande Cadence de Tir (GCT) 155mm self-propelled howitzers on the AMX chassis, reflecting Baghdad's need for self-propelled ordnance. The same year saw orders for the Euromissile Roland mobile surface-to-air missile system, with 13 truck-mounted and 100 static launchers, which were delivered between 1982 and 1985, as well as 2,260 missiles. Panhard also shipped 100 ERC-TH anti-armour vehicles with Euromissile HOT UTM-800 turrets under an order placed in 1976. Renault provided TRM-10000 and TRM-900 trucks, while during 1981, the British company Scammell received a £40 million order from Iraq for 200 trucks. Brazil continued to sell to Iraq and in 1981 won a $250 million contract for more Cascaval and Urutu, together with EE-3 Jararaca reconnaissance vehicles and ASTROS 2 MLRS systems. In his desire to expand his forces, Saddam also turned to a new source, and in 1981 placed an order in China for Type 59 MBT, a derivative of the T-55/55.

Officially, the United Kingdom was neutral in the Iran-Iraq War and imposed an arms embargo, which excluded non-lethal materiel, of which £321.9 million was sold in 1980. During 1981, Britain's Racal supplied £750,000 worth of radios to Iraq, which was seeking Jaguar V frequency-hopping transceivers but would receive only Syncal 30 or obsolete BCC-349 sets. In 1981, the Defence Export Sales Organisation (DESO) sought to sell Chieftain MBT and armoured recovery vehicles (ARV) to Iraq via Jordan, which signed a £1.17 million contract for 15 ARV on March 14. The Foreign Office and DESO sought ways to get Chieftain MBTs to Iraq via Jordan, but then Baghdad secured Russian supplies.[17]

Ammunition expenditure for both sides was higher than anticipated, and a document relating to the relatively quiet week of 19-25 April 1981 showed some 182 tonnes was consumed every

A good study of an IRIA trench in Khuzestan (with a shell exploding in the background). As usual, the trench is rather shallow but quite wide. (Albert Grandolini Collection)

day![18] Daily consumption of artillery ammunition for both sides amounted to 6,235 artillery rounds (75155mm), or more than 150 tonnes, together with 204 missiles (13.5 tonnes) from multiple rocket launchers. The situation became acute in January 1981 when stocks fell dangerously low as divisions were firing up to 1,000 rounds per day. Some ammunition for Russian guns was no longer manufactured by the Warsaw Pact, while alternative sources had either limited manufacturing capability or limited stocks. Yugoslavia received a contract for 3,000 130mm and 5,000 152mm shells, Greece agreed to supply 20,000 shells, while Somalia provided ammunition it had received from Egypt. A major potential source was China, but this was initially unreliable and on 31 January, Shanshal informed Saddam their promised shipment of shells was delayed for at least four months. Meanwhile, friendly Middle Eastern states including Jordan, Kuwait, Saudi Arabia and Yemen provided Russian, French and even US artillery.[19]

In all, Iraq was estimated to have received $3.74.2 billion worth of military equipment during 1981, while Iran received some $800 million.[20] The figures are academic, for it is unclear whether these are actual expenditure or merely the face value of the materiel supplied.

By contrast, Iran suffered a general shortage of equipment, ammunition and spares due to her self-created diplomatic isolation. This dammed the flow of supplies not only from the United States but also from the United Kingdom, and meant few front-line artillery battalions were able to deploy their authorized 18 tubes. The average was 15, but as few as 15 percent of these would be serviceable, while air defence units were lucky to have half their weapons serviceable, leading to frequent complaints from brigades about their exposure to enemy air power.[21] European and Asian black market sources of spares and ammunition for Anglo-American equipment were unreliable in terms of quantity and quality, with some dealers providing obsolete or inoperable equipment, while corrupt officials sometimes skimmed money.[22] Moscow slammed the door to Soviet aid following the persecution of Iranian Communists, a rare example of the superpowers being in agreement

US intelligence noted Tehran was seeking new sources of supply for tank spares and artillery ammunition (especially 155mm and 175mm) in Eastern Europe, North Korea and even Israel, while friendly Libya and Syria did what they could. Tripoli provided T-54/55 and T-62 MBT from its inventories, together with some ammunition, while Syria supplied BMP-1, Sagger anti-armour missiles and 150 launchers for Grail surface-to-air missiles, with three missiles per launcher. Libya placed an order in North Korea on Iran's behalf for its version of the T-62 (Ch'onma-hos), as well as artillery, but Pyongyang's northern neighbour, China, would prove Iran's biggest supplier and won a $2 billion contract for Type 59 tanks, Type 59-I towed 130mm guns and, reportedly, Shenyang F-6 fighters.

Only in small arms was the Iranian situation adequate, and throughout the war there were no reports of Iranian infantry lacking such equipment. Iranian operations, therefore, were based largely upon their infantry, although their superior artillery would also play a key role throughout the year, the superiority in self-propelled ordnance allowing them to concentrate fire rapidly and force the Iraqi batteries to disperse along a broad front, leaving them short of firepower at critical moments.[23]

An interesting view of an IRGC-operated observation post and an RPG-team in western Khuzestan in 1981. (Albert Grandolini Collection)

Table 1: Major Orders by Iraq

Order placed	Country	Equipment			Deliveries
		Type	Model	No	
1980	Brazil	Recon	EE-9	35	1980–1981
		APC	EE-11	148	1982–1984
	East Germany	MBT	T-54/55	50	1981–1982
	Poland	MBT	T-54/55	400	1981–1982
	Yugoslavia	Towed art'ry	76155mm	100	1980–1981
1981	Austria	Towed art'ry	GHN-45	200	1981–1986
	Brazil	Recon	EE-9	200	1982–1985
		APC	EE-11	100	1982–1984
		Recon	EE-3	280	1984–1985
		MLRS	Astros 2	67	1984
	China	MBT	Type 59	300	1982–1984
	Czechoslovakia	MBT	T-55	200	1982–1985
		ICV	BMP-1	750	1981–1987
	Egypt	MBT	T-55	250	1981–1983
		APC	Walid	100	1981
		Towed art'ry	130mm	100	1981–1982
	France	SP Arty	GCT	83	1983–1985
	Poland	MBT	T-55	200	1982–1985
	USSR	MBT	T-72	500	1982–1990
		MBT	T-62	2,150	1982–1989
		ICV	BMD	10	1981
		Towed art'ry	130mm	580	1982–1987
		SP arty	Gvozdika	50	1982–1984
		SP arty	Akatsiya	50	1982–1984
		MLRS	BM-21	200	1983–1984

Table 2: Major Orders by Iran

Order Placed	Country	Equipment			Deliveries
		Type	Model	No	
1980	China	MLRS	Type 63	300	1981–1987
1981	China	MBT	Type 59	300	1982–1984
		Towed art'ry	130mm	300	1982–1984
	North Korea	MBT	T-62	150	1982–1985
		Towed art'ry	130mm	400	1982–1985
	Libya	Recon	EE-9	130	1981
		MBT	T-54/55	125	1981
		MBT	T-62	65	1981
	Syria	ICV	BMP-1	200	1981–1984

Chapter 6 Notes

1. For Iraqi road-building operations, see NTC Iraqi Army, p.149.

Crews of the 92nd Armoured Division posing with their Chieftains during a graduation ceremony, prior to being sent to the front line. Note that most of vehicles in the background have very fresh colours, indicating they were taken out of storage very recently. (Albert Grandolini Collection)

A rear view of a Chieftain Mk.3 from the 92nd Armoured Division. This version was powered by 650hp-strong Leyland L60 engine. Just like the uprated 720hp version that powered Iranian Chieftain Mk.5s, this proved too weak for the task. (Tom Cooper Collection)

2. Tarigh al-Qods is also written Tariq alQuds and Tarigh ol-Qods. An alternative translation is The Path to Jerusalem. Some sources suggest it was also called Karbala 1.
3. For Tarigh al-Qods, see Cooper & Bishop, p.130; *Lessons*, pp.12526, 144 n.14; Malovany, pp.18586; Murray & Woods, p.174 & f/n 16, p.175; O'Ballance, pp.6869; Pollack, pp.19596; Ward, pp.25556; US AISC, p.5-29, 5-36, Fig. 5-11; Imposed War website. Brigadier General Rashid's article in website www.netiran.com/Htdocs/Clippings/FPolitics/ 960615XXFP01.html.ee; also O'Ballance's article 'Iran vs Iraq: Quantity vs Quality?'. Information from Mr Tom Cooper based on the memoirs of Brigadier General Massoed Bakhtiari.
4. Murray & Woods, p.175.
5. US AISC, p.5-29.
6. Op cit, p.5-36.
7. Iranian figures from Imposed War website.
8. O'Ballance, p 78.
9. O'Ballance article 'Iran vs Iraq: Quantity vs Quality?'.
10. CRRC SH-MISC-D-000-827, pp.4748. By late April, the 130mm guns could fire only two or three rounds a day. Murray & Woods, Table 5.1.
11. CRRC SH-MISC-D-000-827, p.38; SH-SHTP-D-000-856, pp.18, 20. Data in Murray & Woods, Table 5.1, indicates that by April 1981, Yugoslavia had delivered to Iraq up to 100 towed

A TOW-armed AH-1J Cobra (serial 3-4572) passing low over the battlefield, heavily scarred by threads of dozens of armoured and other vehicles. The Iranians made extensive use of TOWs and knocked out thousands of Iraqi armoured vehicles and bunkers during the war, equalling out their weakness in armour. (Farzin Nadimi Collection)

artillery pieces; M48 76mm mountain guns, M56 105mm and M65 155mm howitzers.

12. The factory began production in 1984.

13. For arms sales to both sides, see Foss, various years; De Lestapis, pp.109–12; SIPRI year books; IISS Military Balance; US AISC, p.535.

14. See Bani-Sadr's comments upon Iran's self-imposed isolation from the international community in Murray & Woods, p.97.

15. Pelletiere, p.74.

16. O'Ballance, p.103; Pelletiere, p.45. However, the actual price may have been under $230 million. See CRRC SP-PDWN-D-000-552; DIA DDB-2680-103-88.

A famous photo of an Iraqi Mi-25 thundering low over BMP-1s of an armoured unit in western Khuzestan, early on during the Iran-Iraq War. The Mi-25 was a fast, well-armed and well-protected helicopter, that could not hover and had to be flown like a fighter aircraft. In the words of a former Iraqi pilot flying the type against Iran, 'it felt like being the biggest target over the battlefield'. (Albert Grandolini Collection)

17. UK NA FCO 8/2845, 8/3841, 8/4156, 8/4162, 8/4164. The Iraqis sought 320–420 new tanks with Cobham armour, 21 ARVs and up to 30 AVLB, together with 500 FH 70 towed 155mm howitzers. The British prevaricated because they did not want Soviet intelligence to inspect the latest Western armour. This prevarication, the high prices demanded by London and the slow delivery of parts to refurbish the captured tanks caused the Iraqis to lose interest, and in December 1981 the exasperated Director of Armour, General Salah Askar, allegedly told the British: "We don't want your stupid tanks." *Saddam's Generals*, pp.132–33.

18. SH-GMID-D-001-020, quoted in Murray & Woods, Table 5.1.

19. Murray & Woods, pp.153, 156–57.

20. Schmidt and US Arms Control and Disarmament Agency study on World Military Expenditures and Arms Transfers.

21. DIA DDB-1100-342-86, p.39.

22. Murray & Woods, pp.162–63; Ward, p.256.

23. For comments on Iranian operations, see US AISC, p.5-30 to 5-33, 5-36.

7
Disaster for Iraq

Despite shortages of equipment, the confidence of Iran's military leaders grew during 1981 as they found solutions to their operational and logistical problems and became more capable at both the tactical and operational levels. The Pasdaran and their clerical supporters were now more willing to co-operate with the IRIA, which itself was willing to bend before the wind, although mutual trust remained skin deep. Inevitably there remained personal and corporate rivalries, yet patriotism meant that the IRIA professionals, regulars and conscripts, together with the Pasdaran and Basij 'amateurs', were now reluctantly willing to work towards the joint goal of driving out the invader.[1] It was a measure of the regime's confidence in the IRIA that it was allowed to create, from late 1981, short-term reservist Qods (Jerusalem) infantry battalions of 500 men, beginning with the 1901st. They were usually assigned to under-strength divisions, especially on the northern and central fronts, which trained them for up to six weeks and retained them for a maximum of 18 months before they were disbanded, then reformed with new personnel.[2]

Yet there remained formidable problems in exploiting the country's huge reserves of manpower. Command and control was hindered by a continued shortage of experienced staff officers, while at brigade level and above, many formations were led by officers propelled beyond their experience or abilities. There was also a shortage of experienced non-commissioned officers (NCOs), the oil in all armed forces, while the revolution continued to undermine military discipline for, despite Khomeini's strictures, many clerical commissars continued to question and even countermand officers' orders.[3]

Communications were hamstrung by a severe shortage of radios and field telephones. Before the revolution, each division had 2,000 radio sets, but the expansion of the Pasdaran and the perennial shortage of spares reduced availability as the regime trawled the world's markets for replacements. There was always considerable HF traffic, especially for logistics and movements, as well as between the front and higher commands. Even if the enemy could not decrypt the signals, the level of traffic alerted them that an offensive was imminent. As the Iranians became aware of their communications security problem, they made greater use of multi-channel radios as well as landline communications, while couriers were also used extensively.[4]

As the winter rains eased, the Iranians prepared to drive out the invader and launched their first blow in March 1982 around Dezful in Operation Fath-ol Mobin, which proved a devastating success and even sucked in Iraq's 3rd Arm Div from the Karun front.[5] To pre-empt this attack, divert enemy reserves and boost his prestige, Saddam demanded an offensive towards Bostan.[6] As 14th Inf Div had lost Bostan, it was now given the opportunity to regain its honour by retaking the town using the 10th Arm Div's 17th Arm and 24th Mech Bdes, 3rd Arm Div's 12th Arm Bde, 18th and 108th Inf Bdes, as well as the 1st and 8th Popular Army Special Missions (PASM) Bdes. A frontal assault supported by 12 artillery battalions (200 guns) was launched by 24th Mech Bde/10th Arm Div at dawn on 6 February in rain which turned the battlefield into a swamp. The defenders, Pasdaran supported by the reinforced 3rd Bde/92nd IRIA Arm Div, and four self-propelled artillery battalions augmented by a towed battery (80 guns), resisted fiercely, using a berm outside Bostan as the MLR.

On his own initiative, the 6th Arm Div commander (General Mahmood Shukur, the former 10th Arm Bde commander) sent his 25th Mech Bde northward towards Sableh on a raid which captured six Chieftain MBT but did not cause the defenders much trouble.[7] Reinforcements were rushed from Dezful to Bostan, but the Iraqi attack was never a serious threat and ended three days later after gaining little ground, although the Popular Army formations were reported to have distinguished themselves. The operation did, however, force the Iranians to consume much of the artillery ammunition assembled for the Dezful offensive and allowed the Iraqis to strengthen the defences east of Al Amarah.

Iraqi morale was boosted, but Saddam was unhappy and demoted some officers while augmenting the artillery train to renew battle on 13–14 February, then again on 20 March. But the continued muddy conditions prevented any progress, and hopes of renewing the operation when the ground dried were dashed two days later when the Iranians launched their own offensive.

The success of Tarigh al-Qods, followed by Fath-ol Mobin, saw new dissensions within the Iranian leadership. The rift was within the IRIA, but also between it and the Pasdaran, with old wounds reopened by the Ghotbzadeh Plot. Former Foreign Minister Sadiq Ghotbzadeh was arrested on 9 April, accused of planning Khomeini's assassination, and would publicly admit his guilt. He also implicated the IRIA, which led to a new purge and by mid-August 70 officers had been shot.[8]

Against this background, Rezai and the Pasdaran argued in the SDC in simplistic terms against the IRIA's set-piece combined-arms operation, which required substantial materiel support, whose assembly took time. They downplayed the role of the IRIA and emphasized how the Pasders' fervour had carried them through the enemy defences and deep into their rear. They wished to strike the moment the ground was dry enough in southern Khuzestan, removing the external threat to the regime, which could then focus upon the internal one and complete the Islamic Revolution. Shirazi and Zahirnejad urged delay so the offensive would have adequate support, but Defence Minister Salimi, excited by the success at Dezful, overruled them.

Planning for Operation Beit-ol-Mogaddas (Sacred House, a Koranic name for Jerusalem) began in late February or March, but intensified during April under the direction of General Rahim Safavi.[9] There was an intense reconnaissance effort conducted by the Pasdaran and much of 23rd SF Bde, reinforced by a naval commando and four IIG companies, to detect weaknesses in the enemy defences. In these missions, the scouts exploited their superior night-fighting equipment acquired by the Shah.[10] They received local help, notably exploring the Darkhovin Salient, where they were aided by the local Arab Bani-Kar tribe, a telling indictment of Iraqi political failure. COMINT helped to fill out the intelligence picture, while the IRIAF deployed photographic reconnaissance and SIGINT squadrons, and twice used Unmanned Aerial Vehicles.[11]

The Iraqi enclave in Khuzestan was bounded by the Karkheh Kur in the north, the Shatt al-Arab in the south, the Hawizah Marshes in the west and the Karun in the east. The Iraqis had again blocked irrigation ditches during the winter rains to flood large areas in front of their defences, notably between the Karkheh and the Karkheh Kur, east of the Susangerd-Hoveyzeh line, as well as along 55km of the Karun's western bank a few kilometres north of Darkhovin, this inundation lapping along on the Ahvaz-Khorramshahr highway.

An interesting study of an Iranian Chieftain, the crew of which increased its protection by adding sand-bags to the top of the turret and the front of the hull. Such measures became necessary when the type proved vulnerable to APFSDS hits from Iraqi T-72s and HOT anti-tank missiles fired by Iraqi helicopters but also as additional protection against Iraqi artillery. (Tom Cooper Collection)

T-62s and T-55s of an Iraqi armoured company somewhere in the Dezful area, shortly before Iran launched Operation Beit-ol-Mogaddas. A standard armoured company of an Iraqi armoured division had 11 MBTs (it seems that by early 1982 some Iraqi units were so short of T-62s that they also had to use T-55s), a BTR-60 for the command team and at least one BTS-3 armoured recovery vehicle attached (one of the latter visible in the left foreground). (Albert Grandolini Collection)

Starting in 1982, the IrAAC began combining its Mi-25s and SA.342 Gazelles into hunter-killer teams: Mi-25s would saturate the target zone with unguided rockets and machine-gun fire, after which the more vulnerable Gazelles would try to target Iranian armour or fortifications with HOT anti-tank guided missiles. (Albert Grandolini Collection)

Sudanese volunteers on parade before being sent to the front. Several contingents of foreign workers were coerced to serve with the Iraqi Army during the war with Iran, but there were volunteers too. Among these were about 3,000 Jordanian members of the al-Yarmouk Force, the battalions of which were assigned to the 7th and 15th Infantry Divisions. They proved of poor quality and some even mutinied. All Jordanians were withdrawn by 1983. (Albert Grandolini Collection)

The 65km northern face was anchored west of Hoveyzeh on the River Noisan and in the west by Dub-e Said. East of Hoveyzeh it overlooked flooded land, apart from the 'land bridge' south-west of Tarrah, while the northern part of the 105km eastern defences, which followed the Ahvaz-Khorramshahr highway, also covered inundations, with major strongpoints at Hamid and Ahu. South-east of Ahu, and the southern edge of the flooded area, the river meanders eastward, twisting and turning for some 20km before straightening out near Darkhovin and running south-west to the Shatt.

The Iraqi line here bulged outwards to form the Darkhovin Salient, which encompassed a small stream, shown on Soviet maps as Nakhr Peyen, which ran from near Hoseyniyeh (also written Hoseinieh or Hosseinieh) north-east through an area of prehistoric settlements, of which only earthen mounds (tels) remained. Behind was the desert, with numerous natural obstacles to aid the defence, along with minor roads and tracks, often on embankments, while west-to-east obstacles to movement in the southern part of the salient included abandoned irrigation canals and river channels.[12]

To overcome these obstacles, Tehran assembled some 135,000 troops, half of them Pasdaran and Basij, with some 350 tanks, 100 self-propelled and towed guns, 40 MLRS and 26 Cobra gunships, as the revolution's sword was raised to cut off the invader's hand. Safavi envisaged enveloping the enclave, and on 20 April assembled three task forces (Gharargah): Qods opposite the northern face, Fath on the upper Karun and Nasr on the lower Karun, together with an IRIAF forward headquarters at Vahdati AFB under Colonel Bahram Houshyar. In addition to their own troops, the task forces could count upon the 22nd and 55th Artillery Groups, with some 20 artillery battalions and seven MLRS batteries.

Task Force Qods would pin down the forces on the northern face along three axes. West of Hoveyzeh, 1st Bde/16th IRIA Arm Div (minus a tank battalion but with three Pasdaran battalions and two IIG companies) would demonstrate as 2nd Bde advanced upon Hoveyzeh. Meanwhile, the 58th Malek-e Ashtar Pasdaran Bde, which was boosted to double strength like the other Pasdaran units, would make a separate thrust across the Tarrah 'land bridge' to storm the enemy defences, supported by a Special Forces battalion and 3rd Bde/16th Arm Div.

Simultaneously, the main blow would be launched around Darkhovin, the boundary between Task Forces Fath and Nasr, at the

IRGC troops approaching an olive grove near Khorramshahr. Poorly trained and equipped, but highly motivated and zealous, they eventually developed into a force the Iraqi generals feared the most. (Farzin Nadimi Collection)

Both sides made extensive use of Soviet-made BM-21 multiple rocket launcher systems, ammunition supplies permitting. The 40-tube system could fire 70kg heavy rockets to a range of about 20km. This was one of dozens of examples operated by the Iranians. (Tom Cooper Collection)

then isolate and destroy the Ahvaz Salient and up to three enemy divisions, but what if the Iraqis exploited the road network between the Hawizah Marshes and the Karun to escape across the border? Khomeini opposed any crossing of the frontier, even in 'hot pursuit', and while pressure was mounting on him to change his mind, this remained official policy, which meant the enemy would have a sanctuary. If Qods could not pin down the northern face, then Safavi's prime objective might not be achieved. He was more confident of achieving the second part, for while part of Nasr put pressure on the Khorramshahr bridgehead, the remainder, with Fath, would drive south to take the border town of Shalamcheh and isolate Khorramshahr.

The IRIAF had achieved air superiority in the two previous offensives and Safavi hoped it would repeat this feat, despite being severely understrength, with only 20 strike aircraft (F-4 and F-5) available for what it dubbed Operation Shahbah 3 (Phantom 3), plus reconnaissance and transport units. However, three fighter squadrons (F-14) were available to shield the Iranian rear, together with surface-to-air missiles three HAWK batteries (two in the Abadan area) and a Rapier battery, while the troops had a significant number of Libyan- and Syrian-supplied Grail man-portable weapons, which they first used in April.

From 7 April, the Iraqis noticed enemy preparations, including 21st Div training with boats, the assembly of bridging equipment as well as the arrival of 22 field hospitals and, 10 days later, the transfer of forces south from the Dezful front (including a tank battalion of 64th Div), and recognized the implications. These were confirmed by an increase in Iranian probes, with a steady rise in raids, artillery bombardments and reconnaissance flights. Baghdad realized that an offensive was imminent and where it would fall, but lacked the power to disrupt it; indeed, the recent Iranian successes left the more thoughtful Iraqi officers contemplating the coming year with growing concern, although its leaders loudly proclaimed confidence.

The new Iranian tactics bewildered even the best Iraqi officers, as General Hamdani later commented to the Americans:

enemy salient on the opposite bank. Fath would would cross in the north at Halub (also Jish Haloub) with 55th IRIA Air Bde, with the Pasdaran 19th Fajr Sar-Allah and 30th Beit-ol-Mogaddas Divs and 59th Zolfaqhar Bde. It would strike up the Nakhr Peyen valley, with the airborne troops covering the right flank, to establish a bridgehead into which would be fed first the IRIA's 92nd Arm Div, then the 37th Arm Bde. These would spearhead a breakout to the west and north-west to cut the Ahvaz-Khorramshahr highway and isolate the Ahvaz Salient. Meanwhile, the infantry-heavy Task Force Nasr would exploit little islands near Mesian to establish a bridgehead with the IRIA 21st Inf Div and the Pasdaran 5th Nasr and 31st Ashura Divs, as well as the 40th IRIA Inf Bde, to shield Fath from relief attempts from the south.

Once Safavi sprung the trap, the two armoured divisions would

In order to counter the threat of the Iraqi armour, the Pasdaran formed motorcycle-mounted teams, with the pillion passenger carrying an RPG-7. Motorcycles also saw widespread use in resupply missions for forward-deployed units. (Albert Grandolini Collection)

Each phase of a military operation is supposed to happen at a certain time (for fire support etc.), but these Iranians had neither phases nor organization. They did not care if they had fire support or anything; they had no concept of command and control, timing etc. They just kept moving they swarmed through our artillery zones, which wrecked our plans and calculations.[13]

This echoed comments by conservative British and French officers on the Western Front in 1918 about German *Schwerpunkt Taktik*, and possibly of their successors in France in May 1940.

Massed infantry assaults, which most armies would have handled with a combination of firepower and mechanized manoeuvre, left the Iraqis bewildered. They were unsure when, or where, to launch the necessary ripostes, and tended to hit the enemy centre rather than striking the flanks, which caused heavy losses to artillery and anti-armour missiles. Iraqi artillery fire arrangements, which should have been based upon flexible plans at brigade level, were too rigid and often dictated by the divisional commander, who had little knowledge of the fluid tactical situation.[14] The Iraqis would begin to discuss the problem only in April 1982, and only a year later did the first doctrinal manuals appear.[15]

In the meantime, the only practical defence was to strengthen the fortifications during the rainy season, which topped up the flooded areas north of the Karkheh Kur and on the western bank of the Karun. Behind them was usually a strong screen of rifle companies, which would be withdrawn to the MLR in the face of a major assault. These positions were behind barbed-wire entanglements and deep minefields, 5th Mech Div alone laying 38,329 mines, of which 11.5 percent were anti-armour versions.[16] The MLR was a kilometre behind and remained upon a buttressed berm, often built with materials from demolished villages, sheltered by more wire entanglements and minefields.

As autonomous company strongpoints had proved too weak, the berms were now buttressed with battalion strongpoints, each holding a 2km section of the line, with two company positions on the MLR and a third, linked by more berms, some 2km behind. Brigade headquarters would have two battalions up and one in reserve 58km from the FEBA, while divisional mechanized reserves were in fortified positions 1520km behind them. The continued shortage of infantry meant that up to half the MLR berm was unmanned and covered only with fire from the battalion strongpoints. For this reason, the Iraqi mechanized forces created company-sized reaction forces, armoured brigades deploying up to 40 tanks and 10 APC, while mechanized brigades had 10 tanks and 40 APC. US intelligence described Iraqi defensive concepts as 'ill-conceived', with open division and brigade flanks (unmanned berms), and armoured units in fixed defences with little infantry support.

The mechanized reaction forces were especially important along the eastern part of the front facing the Karun, where the area east of the Ahvaz-Khorramshahr highway was to be a killing zone for any enemy crossing. The highway embankment had been fortified to act as the MLR, while a screen of fortified observation posts was established along the river bank, with the gaps between them covered by teams of mobile scouts. In most places this killing zone was 1015km deep, but there was a significant weakness near the middle, opposite the Darkhovin Salient, where the killing zone was twice this depth.

With only three infantry brigades to cover this sector, the fortified observation posts would play a significant role in the defence, although some five-metre berms were built to restrict enemy movement after the Karun Bridgehead, which had acted as a breakwater to shelter this salient, was lost in September. The observation points, like those in the Bar Lev Line on the Suez Canal in 1973, would now act to channel any major assault into a killing zone around the Nakhr Peyen valley, which held a gun line, sometimes with fortified fire bases, many around the tels that acted as observation posts.[17]

Considerable effort was expended fortifying the Khorramshahr area, where the southern bridgehead had berms studded with bunkers, observation points and fire posts covering fire zones created by levelling up to a third of the surviving buildings and vegetation. For the first time, the northern part of the town was fortified, with bulldozers and earthmovers levelling buildings and trees to create good fields of fire, then build a 2.5-metre berm which arced across the city, with the Shatt al-Arab at its back, this being nicknamed by some 'The Wall of Persia'.[18] The emphasis, however, was upon repelling attacks from across the river, not along its banks from the

M113s of an Iranian reconnaissance battalion probably that of the 21st Infantry Division waiting for the order to advance during Operation Beit-ol-Mogaddas. (Tom Cooper Collection)

This Iraqi mechanized company was quickly overrun during Operation Beit-ol-Mogaddas, and most of its vehicles including at least four BMP-1s and three OT-62s captured intact. (Tom Cooper Collection)

A blazing Iraqi T-54/55 knocked out by an AH-1J Cobra helicopter with a TOW missile, while attempting to run away from a position about to be overrun by the Iranians. Note the 120mm mortar in the foreground. (Tom Cooper Collection)

north and the significant weak point in the defences where the Karun meandered south-east.

Intelligence was vital to the Iraqi plans, but units were reluctant to send out reconnaissance patrols, while higher level collection and analysis remained major problems until the summer of 1982, partly due to a continued shortage of Farsi-speaking officers. Baghdad pleaded with Jordan and Saudi Arabia for intelligence support, but even then the system was over-centralized; data was first sent to Baghdad for evaluation by the General Headquarters and the GMID. Vital information often did not reach the front line in time, while IrAF reconnaissance photographs often took 48 hours to reach units.[19]

The cloud had a silver lining, for during the autumn of 1981 an Iranian officer defected and brought with him a Crypto C-52 electro-mechanical enciphering machine. With it, the GMID, backed by Soviet KGB technical assistance, began to crack enemy codes and confirmed the enemy build-up in Khuzestan and its support by bridging and ferry units, together with North Korean technical experts.[20]

Yet the Iraqis were probably unaware of either the timing or its ambitious objectives. In March, 3rd Arm Div (now under Kurdish infantry officer Brigadier General Juwad Assad Shetna) was withdrawn from the western bank of the Karun in response to Fath-ol Mobin, but it returned in April in response to the emerging threat, having suffered relatively light losses because it had been used sparingly at Dezful.[21] Its return brought Qadhi's III Corps to five divisions, each swollen to twice the usual size with a total of some 30 brigades, together with 15th Inf Div (Major General Mohammad Abdul Qader) on the Faw Peninsula with 420th and 501st Inf Bdes, 1st PASM Bde and a brigade-size battle group. North of the Shatt, the corps had 90,000 men holding the 215km line in the Hoyehzeh-Ahvaz-Khorramshahr triangle, but it remained AFV–heavy, with the regular infantry severely diluted by reserve, police and Popular Army units. Qadhi had 7501,000 tanks, mostly deployed as tactical level reserves, and the only operational level reserve was 10th Arm Bde, which remained in the Basra area.

The 3rd Arm Div returned to the Darkhovin Salient and had 6th, 12th and 30th Arm, 8th Mech and 19th, 418th and 606th Inf Bdes, the infantry units augmented by battalions of 33rd SF Bde. The 9th Arm Div (Brigadier General Kamil Mishri) shuffled northward opposite the flooded areas of the upper Karun with 14th Mech, 35th and 43rd Arm and 104th Inf Bdes. The northern face of the Ahvaz Salient was held by two divisions: 6th Arm Div in the west, still under Shukur, with 16th and 56th Arm, 25th Mech and 45th, 49th and 90th Inf Bdes; and 5th Mech Div in the east with 15th and 20th Mech, 26th Arm 109th, 419th and 504th Inf Bdes, and battalions of 31st SF Bde. Holding the lower Karun around Khorramshahr was 11th Inf Div (Brigadier General Said Mohammed Fethi) with 22nd, 28th 48th 102nd, 113th, 117th and 502nd Inf Bdes, augmented by a tank battalion and 2nd PASM Bde, as well as the equivalent of a brigade of Border Guards.[22]

By 27 April, the Iraqis had a good idea of both enemy forces and intentions, and at 6:30 p.m. on 28 April the GMID correctly warned the enemy would attack around midnight on 29/30 April and, as also anticipated, the attack would be on all three fronts. The Qods attack west of Hoveyzeh, supported by seven

The Iraqis lost hundreds of MBTs, and even more other vehicles and precious equipment, during Operation Beit-ol-Mogaddas. This group of T-54/55s was knocked out and captured while attempting to shelter inside a palm grove. (Tom Cooper Collection)

This knocked-out T-72 burned out completely after a direct hit set on fire the fuel cells installed above its right fender. Note that the vehicle was still wearing the original olive green colour applied in the USSR before delivery. It is possible that this was 'enhanced' by the addition of some mud, resulting in what looks like a strip of grey colour on the gun tube. (Tom Cooper Collection)

The extent of the Iraqi defeat during Operation Beit-ol-Mogaddas was immense. The heavy equipment left behind by retreating or destroyed Iraqi units was sufficient to equip several new armoured and mechanized brigades of the IRGC. (Tom Cooper Collection)

In an attempt to suppress the activity of IRIAA AH-1 Cobra attack helicopters, the Iraqis began deploying large numbers of ZSU-57-2s along their front lines in 1982. The system was handicapped by a lack of radar control, but its range proved superior to that of the ZU-23, and it was effective against exposed infantry formations too. (Tom Cooper Collection)

An Iraqi OT-64 SKOT APC, knocked out during Operation Beit-ol-Mogaddas. Iraq imported 386 such vehicles from Czechoslovakia in the 1970s, and they seem to have seen active service only during the first two years of the war with Iran. (Tom Cooper Collection)

bridges, established a bridgehead over the Noisan with 2nd Bde/16th Div, but made little progress because the bridges were struck by the IrAF. The Iraqi 6th Arm Div had contained the situation and the news from the neighbouring 5th Mech Div was also encouraging, although neither was aware that within a day the Iranian 1st Bde/16th Div had been quietly withdrawn and sent south.

The 5th Mech Div planned first to contain the Iranian attackers, then drive them back with mechanized reserves which were moving up even as the bombardment began. Yet the superior Iranian artillery pounded its positions with its usual accuracy, and this was exploited by the Pasdaran and Basij with their customary élan. Within two-and-a-half hours, they had made several dangerous penetrations in 109th and 419th Inf Bde's front, but the arrival of the mechanized brigades restored the line by 9:00 a.m. The Iranians desperately called for reinforcements and artillery support, but by late afternoon had been driven back to their start line.

Undaunted, the attacks were renewed with dwindling intensity over the next three days, but even when they forced their way through artillery fire and the obstacle belt, the Iranians were swiftly driven back by counter-attacks. The Iraqi 5th Mech Div claimed to have inflicted 10,000 dead, destroyed five tanks and taken 151 prisoners, while suffering 1,028 casualties, including 176 dead and 357 missing, with losses of 12 tanks, eight APC and six howitzers.[23] Task Force Quds failed to achieve its objective of pinning down the enemy because it had to strike on three independent axes, which would ultimately allow the Iraqis to salvage something from the wreck.

Meanwhile, to the south, a cancer was growing in the weakest point in the Iraqi defences. The main Iranian blow was launched across the 200-metre-wide Karun some 60km south of Ahvaz on both sides of the Darkhovin salient. The sector was under General Assad of 3rd Arm Div, who had earned a high reputation against the Israelis in Syria and then against his own people in 1974.[24] With only three infantry brigades (9,000 men), he had to plan a defence in depth in killing fields far from the Karun, where he would exploit his superior tank strength, some 300 tanks against 200 Iranian.

An Iraqi bivouac overrun by Iranian infantry during Operation Beit-ol-Mogaddas. In the foreground is a BRDM-2, behind it a ZPU-4 anti-aircraft machine gun, while two BTR-60s and a T-62 can be made out in the background. (Albert Grandolini Collection)

Supported by battalions of 23rd SF Bde, the main Iranian crossings were north and south of Darkhovin; Task Force Fath led by Fajr Sar-Allah and 55th Air Bde, while Ashura spearheaded Task Force Nasr. The Iranians exploited the gaps to infiltrate the observation posts and storm those threatening the bridging sites, airborne troops striking those in the north and the Pasdaran those in the south. Engineers then began work throwing three bridges into the Fath bridgehead and two into the Nasr one.[25] The IrAF, which flew 218 fixed-wing sorties that day compared with 20 by the IRIAF, vainly attempted to destroy the bridges, across which Fath began to send 1st and 2nd Bdes of 92nd Div, some 20,000 men, 500 AFVs, 5,000 vehicles and 200 tonnes of ammunition on the first day alone, while Nasr sent two brigades of 21st Div.

A brigadier-general of the Iraqi Army, together with dozens of his troops, most apparently from the Popular Army (al-Jaysh ash-Shabi). Up to 15,000 Iraqi troops were captured during Operation Beit-ol-Moqaddas. (Tom Cooper Collection)

Meanwhile, the IRIA and Pasdaran, with good gunship and light armoured support, pushed the 'shoulders' of the bridgehead along the Karun, while the Fath spearhead drove southwest through the fortified tels, many Pasdaran fighting on foot but led by others in light trucks or even on motorcycles! The Nasr troops had to fight their way westwards across irrigated fields, and despite enemy helicopter attacks they claimed to have cut the highway south of Hoseyniyeh by 11:00 a.m., although they were probably held short of the road. By the end of the day, the Iranians had established a bridgehead some 1425km deep and up to 30km wide, the Americans noting: "The Iranians were able consistently to out-maneuver their opponent during the initial attack."[26]

The speed of the Fath advance was an unwelcome surprise for Assad, disrupting his tactical plan because most of his armour was too far in the rear to aid the battered infantry, who could rely only upon Sagger missiles and RPGs against AFVs. The closest Iraqi formation was 12th Arm Bde, which began a series of desperate and unsupported counter-attacks, but every Iraqi attempt to stand was compromised as the Iranians sliced through Popular Army units like a hot knife through butter. This allowed the Iranians to expand the bridgehead on 1 May, with Fath receiving 37th Arm Bde while the rest of 21st Div joined the Nasr spearhead. Iraqi aircraft ran the gauntlet of Grail missiles and ZSU-23s, which together claimed 16 aircraft, forcing Saddam to order an end to the attacks.

During the afternoon and early evening, 9th Arm Div sent its mechanized reserves south to meet the Iranian threat as Fath regrouped. On the morning of 2 May, the Iranian 92nd Arm Div began pushing northwards in dense fog, which allowed it to infiltrate the three defending brigades but also confused the attackers, who gained ground but were unable to exploit their success.[27] The IrAF

Two IRIA M113s in a laager during the summer of 1982. The type was primarily used by reconnaissance battalions assigned to each Iranian Army division. To keep the troops cool, they brought their vehicles together and then draped a canvas over the two rear doors. (Tom Cooper Collection)

Iranian Brigadier-General Qasem-Ali Zahrinejad gives his presentation on Iranian military successes during Operation Beit-ol-Moqaddas to representatives of the international media in March 1982. Zahrinejad was the Chief of the Joint Staff and Khomeini's representative at the Supreme Defence Council at the time (before that, he served as the Commander of the Iranian Ground Forces).
(Albert Grandolini Collection)

sought to establish air superiority and to interdict the battlefield, but IRIAF fighters and missiles would claim some 4450 of their aircraft.[28] Piecemeal Iraqi counter-attacks against the northern part of the bridgehead continued as Assad brought up his 8th Mech Bde to support 606th Inf Bde, while 9th Arm Div committed 14th Mech Bde, but the Iraqis were steadily pushed back, allowing the enemy to cut the Ahvaz-Khorramshahr highway as Assad tried desperately to organize a co-ordinated response while appealing for reinforcements. By the end of the day, Iraqi intelligence identified eight divisions and a dozen brigades (most of the latter Pasdaran) west of the Karun.

He finally co-ordinated a riposte with 9th Arm Div, and on 3 May, despite fog followed by rain, which obscured vision and put a film of mud on the desert tracks, the two counter-attacked with gunship support. But the attack was poorly executed and conducted on too narrow a front to face tenacious defence, especially from the Pasdaran, who ignored their casualties until 92nd Div parried the Iraqis, who allegedly lost 100 tanks and regained little ground. More ominously, as the battle raged, 1st Bde/16th Arm Div began to enter the Iranian Karun bridgehead and with its aid the attackers regained more territory in the fog and drizzle, and by 4 May were pushing ever closer to the Ahvaz-Khorramshahr highway.

Meanwhile, the Iranians had focused upon the enemy 'choke point' around Shalamcheh and the highway to Ahvez, with the IRIAF interdicting enemy movements, expending 64 tonnes of ordnance in 40 sorties from 27 May. The disruption of enemy communications increased on 3 May when the Iranian 55th Air Bde despatched a company-strong force which landed by helicopter north of Shalamcheh to harass the Ahvaz-Khorramshahr highway.[29]

On 5 May, the 92nd Div broke through on a 25km front, overran Assad's gun line and ended the day in control of the highway between Hamid and Ahu, despite fierce Iraqi air attacks. The threat to the Ahvaz Salient was growing with every hour; the options were to remain like sheep for slaughter or to evacuate it and use the saved forces for a counteroffensive. Qadhi vacillated, aware that Saddam would never forgive him for abandoning such prestigious territory. A solution to his dilemma seemed on offer on 5 May, when his mentor Shanshal arrived at his headquarters. But when Qadhi asked him to select the option of either abandoning the salient or regrouping the forces there for a counter-attack, Shanshal was non-committal. His proximity to Saddam made him even more aware that a decision would be a hot potato, and he only replied: "You are the corps

Iranian artillery played an important role in Operation Beit-ol-Mogaddas largely through destroying enemy positions, but also with counter-battery work. Here, a M109 is in the process of conducting a fire-support mission. (Tom Cooper Collection)

Several Chieftains lining up before another attack during Operation Beit-ol-Mogaddas. The IRIA's success in getting these hefty vehicles across the Karoun River was crucial for the victory, although Iranian officials give all the credit to the IRGC. (Tom Cooper Collection)

commander, you decide."[30]

With Shukur's 6th Arm Div having contained the situation around Hoveyzeh, Qadhi could have switched it south to join the attack around the Darkhovin Salient, leaving 5th Mech Div to exploit the extensive fortifications to hold the northern face. It would have been a gamble but with good odds, yet Qadhi was in an agony of indecision and did nothing except to leave Shukur and 5th Mech Divs holding the northern face of the salient. Mishiri and Assad continued their counter-attacks on 6 May, attempting to drive through the prevailing fog and rain to destroy the bridges supporting Task Force Fath. The conditions for the Iranian defenders were especially favourable, allowing the Pasdaran, with their anti-armour missiles and RPGs, to get close to enemy AFVs and take a steady toll of them, especially, Mishiri whose progress slowed to a snail's pace. This exposed Assad's left to a counter-attack by 92nd Div, which pushed it back. As the Iraqis began to withdraw amid much confusion, the retreat turned into a rout, forcing Mishiri to break off his attack and retreat, although he found it difficult to break contact.

With the Iraqis reeling, the Iranians exploited the situation and during the late evening began the second phase of the offensive. Fath assembled for a breakout during the night in an attempt to isolate 3rd and 6th Arm Divs, and in the morning thrust westwards to Taialyeh and Kushk, spearheaded by 1st Bde/16th Div and 37th Arm Bde, while Nasr made the main drive southwards. The Pasdaran tore a great gap through the collapsing defences, which allowed 1st and 3rd Bdes/92nd Div to advance 17km down the Ahvaz-Khorramshahr highway.[31] Saddam's 'fire brigade', 10th Arm Bde, began counter-attacks but in poor visibility lost a steady trickle of AFVs to Iranian RPGs.

As the weather improved on 7 May, the Iranian juggernaut drove on

The primary Iranian light reconnaissance vehicle was the British-made Scorpion light tank, a squadron of which was assigned to the reconnaissance battalion of each division. Their crews prided themselves on their very fast driving of this 8-ton vehicle over almost any terrain including marshes and especially on rapid advances into the flanks of Iraqi armoured units. The weak spot of the Scorpion was its gasoline fuel, which was rather rare around the front lines during the war. (Tom Cooper Collection)

A dense column of IRIA and IRGC vehicles about to cross a pontoon bridge on the way to Abadan in spring 1982. (Albert Grandolini Collection)

Jofeyr), the thrust westward was too slow, probably because the bulk of supplies were funnelled southward, and during the day, 6th Arm, 9th Arm and 5 Mech Divs retreated through Taialyeh (also Shabhabi) and Kushk into Iraq, the two villages falling the next day.

Meanwhile, the Iranian 92nd Div advanced south, pushing back the infantry elements of 6th Arm Div (45th and 49th Inf Bdes), destroying Assad's 6th Arm Bde and outflanking the left of 11th Inf Div (48th Bde), as well as relieving the heliborne troops of 55th Bde. Throughout the night, 10th Arm, 48th and 90th Inf Bdes fought desperate rearguard actions, although the last may have been destroyed in the process while infantry formations were ordered into Khorramshahr. The Iranians also needed more infantry, and 6,000 men of 1st and 2nd Bdes/77th Div were flown from Mashad to Omidiyeh air base near Ahvaz during the night 9/10 May in Boeing 747s to break a world record for the number flown in a single aircraft with 1,430.[32] At midnight on 9/10 May, the Iranians began to pin down 11th Inf Div with an attack on southern Khorramshahr.

By 10 May, the Iranians were approaching Shalamcheh, which

and four Iraqi brigades were routed. The GMID warned this exposed 6th Arm and 5th Mech Divs, and forced Qadhi to bite the bullet and order them to withdraw to the south-west, covered by 9th Arm Div. The divisions retreated 30km on the first day, and in announcing the decision on 8 May, Baghdad claimed it was 'to reinforce forces to the south'. Saddam finally recognized the danger and ordered the retreating troops into Khorramshahr, where they were joined by 15th Inf Div's 420nd Bde in what the Iraqi leader ominously announced would be a new Stalingrad. Yet the Iraqi Army was falling apart and the defence increasingly relied upon air power; on this day alone, Saddam's Falcons flew 155 fixed-wing and 98 rotary-wing sorties, causing the IRIAF to move a Hawk battery close to the Darkhovin bridgehead on 8 May.

Task Force Qods stepped up the pressure, and 2nd Bde/16th Div isolated Hoveyzeh on 9 May, although the latter village reportedly held out until 18 May, but it was too late and the Iranians had to recognize the enemy were escaping the trap. Although Fath sent troops north to take Hamid and the abandoned Iraqi supply base at Jeghir (also

fell at 10:00 a.m. as artillery and mortar fire set the riverside palm groves ablaze. The 2nd Bde/92nd Div and 55th Air Bde augmented Pasdaran units to secure the town, while Assad tried desperately to retrieve the situation with another armoured counter-attack north of Khorramshahr. But despite strong air support, this had little success and 92nd Division, now reinforced by Fath armoured units, continued to bulldoze the wreckage of the Iraqi Army southwards and the GMID warned the enemy might push into Iraq.

Both sides suffered major logistics problems, which forced the Iraqis to abandon much equipment, the Iranians later claiming to have captured some 100 MBTs, 150 other AFVs and up to 100 guns. But the Iranians in turn began to run out of fuel or ammunition, halting many units; the Iranians would later admit they had not advanced as quickly as they had hoped.[33] Saddam briefly contemplated a counteroffensive using 3rd Arm Div, elements of 9th Arm Div and the newly arrived 7th Inf Div, but the battered armoured division was too weak, and while there was some probing, the Iraqi leader was ultimately understandably reluctant to weaken the shield to defend Basra.[34] Perhaps he was also encouraged by the slowing of the enemy advance, and after he cancelled this plan the Iraqis cobbled together a line covering the Basra-Abadan highway as the Iranians deliberately remained on their side of the frontier.

With commendable foresight, Saddam had begun in April to strengthen defences east of Basra. The water barrier of the Fish Lake had shielded the city since President Bakr's time, but now work began on developing strongpoints across the Basra-Abadan highway, using army engineers and civilians mobilized by the Basra Council. In addition, work began on strengthening the frontier defences, but to gain time and retain the only substantial gain of the 1980 campaign, Saddam was determined to hold Khorramshahr. He was also alarmed at the collapse of Iraqi morale and ordered any soldier fleeing from the battlefield to be shot, a counter-productive action which may actually have encouraged his troops to surrender.

On 13 May, the SDC sought Khomeini's permission to cross the border, but Zahirnejad told a reporter the Ayatollah vetoed it.[35] Yet the issue was clearly not going away, and on 19 May President Khamenei chaired a night-time meeting of the SDC in which the pleas for cross-border operations were underlined by Iraqi counter-attacks earlier in the day by 46th Mech and 38th Arm Bdes/12th Arm Div and 14th Arm Bde/9th Arm Div, joined by 37th Arm Bde/12th Arm Div the following day. To hold the ground, IRIA engineers dug berms which the attackers were unable to overcome, and the defenders' tank-hunting groups claimed 58 AFVs. Underpinning the Iranian border defences were 16th Arm Div south of Jeghir (later reinforced by 37th Arm Bde) and the 92nd Div shielding the Hoseyniyeh area. The 21st Div was around Shalamcheh with up to five Pasdaran brigades, and was joined by 40th IRIA Inf Bde.

That day, GMID warned Saddam that the defences of Khorramshahr facing the new threat lacked both minefields and wire, and those which had been built were not covered by fire. While the Pasdaran were willing to rush the Khorramshahr defences, even they recognized the need for supplies and replacements, and assembling them took a fortnight. This gave the IRIA a fortnight

Members of a successful IRIA TOW-team posing in front of their M151 MUTT jeep, after surviving a sharp clash with withdrawing Iraqis, east of Basra, in summer 1982. (Tom Cooper Collection)

Whenever the Iranians or Iraqis reached a new position, their engineers would rapidly erect up to 3-metre-high berms of sand or earth (often combined with anti-armour ditches in front of them). These Iranian troops have further 'modified' their berm with several shallow foxholes, dug out just behind its top. (Albert Grandolini Collection)

to prepare support for the assault upon the city, which was held by 40,000 men under Fethi's 11th Inf Div. The division had a tank and a reconnaissance battalion, but command and control was impossible for the divisional headquarters was in Iraq and had to control a reported 15 brigades, a figure which may include Border Guard units, within the city.[36]

The defences in the southern arc, facing Abadan, were strong, while those in the northern and western arc were weak, although 11th Inf Div vigorously acted to improve them while also laying carpets of giant caltrops and cars upended vertically in open areas to prevent any heliborne assault. But as Cordesman observed in *The Lessons of Modern War*, "Khorramshahr had become more of a trap for Iraq than a fortress", resembling Hitler's *Festungs* in which so much of the German Army was sacrificed.[37] A pontoon bridge across the Shatt into the south-west corner linked the city with the outside

The Iranians quickly rushed to service a number of ZSU-57-2s captured from Iraqis, and these provided good service against Iraqi attack helicopters. (Tom Cooper Collection)

A column of T-55s only recently captured from the Iraqis and then rushed to service by the IRGC advancing in the direction of Basra in summer 1982. (Albert Grandolini Collection)

world, but this soon came under artillery fire and little in the way of reinforcement or sustenance could be expected over it.

Fath began the task of crushing the last pocket of enemy-held territory, and during a thunderstorm on the night of 20/21 May, struck from the west to cut the link with the pontoon bridge and push the enemy tighter into their tomb. This set the scene for a full-scale assault upon the city two nights later, Nasr striking down the Karun and from Abadan while Fath pushed from the west, both attacks spearheaded by Pasdaran with IRIA artillery and armour. The GMID warned of the imminent attack involving 77th Div on 22 May, and it was launched through the rain during the night of 22/23 May, with the Pasders and Basij trading corpses for metres in a 'human wave' assault. By dawn, the bridge across the Karun linking northern and southern Khorramshahr was in Iranian hands and Nasr was mopping up, Popular Army and Border Guard units readily surrendering. Meanwhile, Fath made steady progress through the weaker western defences, driving the increasingly demoralized defenders into the old town, while Iraqi batteries had great difficulty locating targets amid the ruins. Fethi tried to arrange an evacuation, but it was impossible, and many defenders sought to escape across the Shatt in boats, small craft and even rafts, while others tried to swim to safety, only to drown. In despair, thousands surrendered on the morning of 24 May. By the end of the day, the city was in Iranian hands, together with 12,000–13,000 prisoners and 56 AFVs.[38] Some 2,000 Iraqis were allegedly executed for rape.[39]

The offensive had recovered 5,480km² of Iranian territory and taken 25,400 prisoners, as well as 200 tanks, 250 other AFVs (250 AFVs were destroyed) and 300 guns. As one commentator noted: "It was the greatest feat of Iranian arms since the eighteenth century."[40] But it was costly, with some 30,000 casualties (22 percent), including at least 4,500 dead, although one source has suggested, with considerable exaggeration, a figure of 110,000, including 60,000 dead.[41] The booty did permit the Pasdaran to begin creating artillery batteries, and there were sufficient tanks for them to create two armoured brigades.[42]

The Iranians achieved a spectacular victory by making virtue out of necessity, and US intelligence considered that, with better logistics and

Pasdaran taking cover from the simmering heat in the little shadow provided by a recently captured BMP-1, somewhere east of Basra, in summer 1982. See the colour section for details about this vehicle. (Tom Cooper Collection)

especially transport, the Iranians might have reached Basra, although this was never Tehran's intention. It noted: "Iran's main asset was the dedicated, fearless Pasdaran prepared to suffer incredible hardships and losses."[43] Many commentators have emphasized this point and assumed the Iranian victory was due purely to them burying the enemy in bodies through 'human wave' assaults. But while the Pasdar were notoriously careless with their lives, they were not reckless, and massed infantry assaults were usually directed at night with great precision at positions which had been infiltrated and isolated.[44] The Iranians also had excellent heavy-weapon support despite problems with the resupply of ammunition. Their artillery continued to be superior, with the self-propelled artillery unmatched in the Iraqi Army through its ability to be rapidly concentrated at crucial points.

Iranian air power also proved important, with US intelligence noting:

The Iranians also became adept at using heliborne forces to insert units to capture key positions in advance of their offensives. They also used TOW-equipped Cobra helicopters in close air support missions to compensate for their lack of armour. This strategy was effective against the Iraqis, and vice versa, because both lacked, or did not employ effectively, air defence resources to suppress helicopters or other forms of close air support.[45]

Despite being numerically inferior to the IrAF, the IRIAF played a small, but important, role in the victory, mostly by achieving air superiority. Of the 1,083 combat sorties, nearly 86 percent were combat air patrol, but they claimed 55 victories to aircraft and missiles. Only 12 percent of sorties (130) were close air support or battlefield interdiction, but total losses were only four aircraft. The IRIAF also flew 315 air refuelling and 847 transport sorties in support of the offensive.[46] The IrAF is reported to have flown more than 1,200 sorties between 30 April and 12 May, while the IrAAC flew half that number, but flew some 80 sorties a day up to mid-May.

The greatest Iraqi defeat of the war saw heavy losses in the air matched by those on the ground. US intelligence estimated the Iraqis had suffered 15,000 casualties, while others suggest 30,00050,000. The Iraqi Army strength certainly fell from 210,000 to 150,000, but this was also the result of the Dezful defeat.[47] The complacent belief in the Iraqi Army's technical superiority was a major factor in shaping the defeat, for it restricted its ability to adapt to a changing battlefield situation. Instead of rigidly defending every metre of the 500km line, it should have sought to exploit its numerical superiority in armour to fight deep defensive battles at the operational level. But few of its corps and divisional commanders possessed the confidence to seek this strategy, especially in the face of Saddam's blind obstinacy to hold all the captured terrain. Most were selected for their political reliability rather than military capability and were in a straitjacket of a rigidly hierarchical command structure, answerable to Saddam himself. Iraqi air support was also inferior to Iran's, although there had been improvements in airground co-operation, notably with helicopters, yet problems remained with co-ordination.[48]

Saddam was shocked and angry at the defeat in Khorramshahr. The first to feel the weight of Saddam's wrath were III Corps commander Qadhi, the Kurdish commander of 3rd Arm Div, Assad, and his subordinate Colonel Masa Abd-al-Jalil, the 12th Arm Bde commander.[49] Their court martial was held in July 1982 in Basra, in front of Defence Minister Khairrallah, Deputy Defence Minister Izzat Ibrahim al-Duri, Saddam's political deputy, party leaders and several senior generals, all of whom were desperate to distance themselves from the catastrophe and demonstrate their loyalty to Saddam. The result resembled a Soviet show trial, one Iraqi general noting: "It was not a regular trial; it was tense with a lot of screaming, yelling and hurling of insults." The result was never in doubt, and all three were shot, possibly followed by another dozen officers, while up to 300 were demoted or dismissed.[50]

A Bell AH-1 Cobra of the IRIAA in its natural environment: hovering only metres above the tops of the nearest palms, searching for a suitable target. Its combination with TOW-ATGMs proved highly effective during the Iran-Iraq War. (Tom Cooper Collection)

An Iraqi MT-LB APC knocked out by a TOW fired from an AH-1 in May 1982. (Albert Grandolini Collection)

In the aftermath, Saddam further restricted the individual initiative of divisional commanders so that only corps commanders could authorize reconnaissance missions.[51] In a further ominous parallel with the Soviet Union, Saddam created Punishment Corps (Fayaliq al-Iqab) which were stationed behind units, ready to execute deserters and those commanders who performed poorly.[52]

Events elsewhere offered the Iraqi leader the opportunity for a face-saving gesture. On 3 June, the Israeli ambassador in London was gunned down by a Palestinian and the incensed Israelis decided to smash the Palestinian Liberation Organization in Lebanon, which they invaded three days later. On 10 June, the RCC offered a unilateral ceasefire which would allow Iraqi and Iranian troops to join forces and fight in Lebanon. Shirazi was willing, and a small force was sent, but the radicals regarded the whole affair as an American conspiracy to save Saddam. On 21 June, Khomeini publicly announced the war would continue, and even ignored Saddam's claim on 29 June to have withdrawn from all Iranian territory so that all Moslem troops could 'assist the Palestinians', because he still retained bridgeheads in Iran.

The recapture of Khorramshahr had emboldened Iran, and the euphoria which followed encouraged hardliners, led by Parliament's Speaker, Akbar Hashemi-Rafsanjani, but including Shirazi and Rezai, to argue for the expansion of Iranian war operations into Iraq. Rafsanjari set out Iran's terms for a ceasefire, including Baghdad's admission that it had started the war, the payment of a $100 billion indemnity, reaffirmation of the Algiers Agreement as well as the removal of Saddam and his trial for war crimes. Predictably it was rejected, as the pragmatic Rafsanjani probably expected.

Saddam's gamble had gone horribly wrong, for far from leading to a collapse of the theocracy in Tehran, the invasion had strengthened its authority and now his own regime was under threat. Within six weeks of the loss of Khorramshahr, the Iranians took the war to their enemy with a massive assault towards Basra. The war would continue for another eight years, and when it ended the lines were almost the same as when the Iraqis invaded.

Chapter 7 Notes

1. US AISC, pp.5-30, 5-34, 5-33, 5-36.
2. DIA DDB-1100-343-85, pp.6, 12.
3. For Iranian military problems, see US AISC, pp.5-30 to 5-33. Website AllRefer.com, Country Study and Country Guide, Iran.
4. DIA DDB-1100-342-86, p.35.
5. This will be dealt with in the Northern-Central front book.
6. For this operation, see *Lessons*, pp.12829; Malovany, pp.19091; O'Ballance, p.78; US AISC, pp.6-1, 6-3.
7. Information from General Makki.
8. *Lessons*, p.142; O'Ballance, pp.8990.
9. The operation, also written Bait-al-Mugaddas and Beit olMoqaddass, is sometimes referred to by another Islamic name for Jerusalem, Quds or Holy Quds.
10. These were NVS-700 Night Vision Goggles, an export version of the AN/PVS-4 with Gen 2 Image Intensifiers.
11. Cooper & Bishop, p.130. Bizarrely, Shirazi would tell a ceremony at Ahvaz on 25 May 25 that "It was the first operation in which we had no intelligence reports on the enemy."
12. For Beit-ol-Mogaddas, see Buchan, pp.35253; Cooper & Bishop, pp.130, 13234, 136; Hills, p.14; Farrokh, pp.362, 36567; Hiro, pp.55, 5960, 62, 634; *Lessons*, pp.129, 135140, 142, 147; Malovany, pp.199207; Marashi & Salama, p.146; Murray & Woods, pp.63 f/ n48, 17576,18485 & f/n 46; Nejad, pp.1921; O'Ballance, pp.79, 8285, 89; Pelletiere, p.42; Pollack, pp.19899. Ward, pp.257258; *Saddam's Generals*, pp.16, 3133, 35, 36, 39, 114; *Project 1946*, p.56; US AISC, pp.6-1, 6-3, 6-7, 6-10, Fig. 6-1; SH-GMID-D-000-531.See also O'Ballance article 'Iran vs Iraq'. Summary of World Broadcasts; Foreign Broadcast Information Service. Website Imposed War; Michael Connell on Iranian operational decision-making on website www.dtic.mil/dtic/tr/fulltext/u2/a585872.pdf. I would especially like to thank General Makki for his help and comments.
13. *Saddam's Generals*, pp.3435.
14. DIA DDB-1100-343-85, pp.3132, 55.
15. Murray & Woods, p.181 f/n 39.
16. For Iraqi defences, see Murray & Woods, pp.18081; DIA DDB-1100-343-85, pp.5758.
17. The Bar Lev Line observation points were some 30km from the Lateral Road, the jump-off point for Israeli armoured counter-attacks, which were thwarted by anti-armour missiles carried by the Egyptian infantry.
18. O'Ballance, pp.8485.
19. DIA DDB-1100-343-85, pp.5051.
20. Murray & Woods, pp.7071.The intelligence appreciations shown in SH-GMID-D-000-531 clearly are based upon this source. Once again, I would like to thank Mr Ralph Simpson and Mr Reuvers for their advice. The price of KGB support was the delivery of a damaged Iranian F-4 Phantom.
21. Information from General Makki.
22. The 102nd, 104th, 109th, 113th and 117th Bdes were all former police formations. Information from Pesach Malovany.
23. Murray & Woods, pp.18083. The Iraqis call this action the Fourth Battle of Khafajiah.
24. *Saddam's Generals*, pp.33, 35.
25. The Shah received Bailey Bridges from Britain, seven M4T6 pontoon bridges from the United States and ribbon bridges from Germany. In addition, US intelligence estimated he received from the USSR five to eight PMP, 6570 GSP and 6065 TMM. DIA DDB-2680-103-88, Part II, pp.1213.
26. US AISC, p.6-28.
27. A contemporary Iraqi broadcast said there was a sandstorm.
28. Cooper & Bishop, pp.13233, 136.
29. During the offensive, IRIAA transport helicopters moved 3,561 troops, mostly reinforcements for the front line, and 101 tonnes of supplies, mostly ammunition.
30. *Saddam's Generals*, p.114.
31. Some sources suggest that part of this force inadvertently penetrated a kilometre into Iraq.
32. See Cooper & Bishop, p.134. The 3rd Bde was reported by 18 May to be attached to 92nd Div with an M47 tank battalion. SH-GMID-D-000-531.
33. O'Ballance, p.84.
34. US AISC, p.6-10. Information from General Makki.
35. Iranian broadcast of 17 May.
36. Murray & Woods, p.178. See also Cooper & Bishop, p.133; O'Ballance, p.84, says the garrison had three divisions and three brigades.
37. *Lessons*, p.138. O'Ballance, p.84.
38. The Iranians claimed to have taken 19,000 prisoners at Khorramshahr, but US AISC, p.6-10, probably based upon COMINT and satellite images, puts the figure at 12,000.
39. Entry on Khorammashahr on answers.com website. The figure is surprising, given that most women, girls and boys had been evacuated in 1980.
40. Buchan, p.353.
41. *Lessons*, p.142.
42. Not divisions, as in O'Ballance, p.106.
43. US AISC, p.6-28.
44. Op cit, p.6-29.
45. Op cit, p.6-28. This last statement is at odds with comments from other sources about the growing effectiveness of Iranian air defence assets, notably the Grail missiles. The IRIAA lost only four helicopters in this campaign and expended 39 TOW. Copper & Bishop, p.134.
46. Cooper & Bishop, pp.13334.
47. *Lessons*, p.140; Murray & Woods, p.185; US AISC, pp.6-10, 6-28. Hiro, p.60, says the IrAF was reduced to 100 serviceable combat aircraft.
48. US AISC, pp.6-27, 6-28, 6-29.
49. For the military purge, see Marashi & Salama, p.146; Murray & Woods, p.184 & f/n.
50. *Saddam's Generals*, pp.33, 3536; *Project 1946*, p.56.
51. *Saddam's Generals*, p.36.
52. Marashi & Salama, p.146.

Army Orders of Battle, September 1980

ISLAMIC REPUBLIC OF IRAN ARMY

Western Iran
Azerbaijan Province
64th Infantry Division (Urmia)
1st (Urmia), 2nd (Salmas), 3rd (Naqadeh) Infantry Brigades
Kordistan Province
28th Infantry Division (Sanandaj)
1st (Sanandaj), 2nd (Saqqez), 3rd (Marivan) Infantry Brigades
Kermanshah Province
81st Armoured Division (Kermanshah)
1st (Kermanshah), 2nd (Hashabad), 3rd (Sar-e Pol-e Zahab) Armoured Brigades
4th (Sar-e Pol-e Zahab) Mechanized Brigade
Khuzestan Province
92nd Armoured Division (Ahvaz)
1st (Ahvaz), 2nd (Dezful), 3rd (Hamidiyeh) Armoured Brigades
22nd Independent Artillery Group (Ahvaz)
Oresian Province
84th Infantry Brigade (Khoramabad)

Central Iran
Qazvin Province
16th Armoured Division (Qazvin)
1st (Qazvin), 2nd (Zanjan), 3rd (Qazvin) Armoured Brigades
Tehran Province
21st Infantry Division (Tehran)
1st, 2nd, 3rd (all Tehran) Infantry Brigades, 4th (Tehran) Armoured Brigade
23rd Special Forces Brigade (Nohed)
33rd Independent Artillery Group (Tehran)
Sharqi Province
40th Infantry Brigade (Sarab)
11th Independent Artillery Group (Maragheh)

South Iran
Fars Province
37th Armoured Brigade (Shiraz)
55th Airborne Brigade (Shiraz)
Esfahan Province
44th, 55th Independent Artillery Groups (Esfahan)

East Iran
Andapan Province
30th Infantry Brigade (Gorgan)

Khorasane Province
77th Infantry Division (Masshad)
1st (Bojnurd), 2nd (Quchan), 3rd (Masshad) Infantry Brigades
Sitan-Va-Baluchestan Province
88th Armoured Brigade (Zahedan)

IRAQI ARMY

I Corps (Kirkuk)
2nd Mountain Infantry Division: 2nd, 4th, 36th Mountain Brigades
4th Mountain Infantry Division: 5th Mountain, 18th, 29th Infantry Brigades
7th Mountain Infantry Division: 19th, 38th, 39th Mountain Brigades
8th Infantry Division: 3rd, 22nd, 23rd Infantry Brigades
11th Infantry Division: 44th, 45th, 48th, 49th Infantry Brigades
12th Armoured Division: 37th, 50th Armoured, 46th Mechanized Brigades
31st Special Forces Brigade
32nd Special Forces Brigade (attached from II Corps)
Headquarters 95th, 97th Reserve Brigades

II Corps (Baghdad)
3rd Armoured Division: 6th, 12th Armoured, 8th Mechanized Brigades
6th Armoured Division: 16th, 30th Armoured, 25th Mechanized Brigades
10th Armoured Division: 17th, 42nd Armoured, 24th Mechanized Brigades
Republican Guard Brigade
10th Armoured Brigade
17th Special Forces Brigade
Headquarters 90th, 93rd, 94th, 96th Reserve Brigades

III Corps (Nasiriya)
1st Mechanized Division: 1st, 27th Mechanized, 34th Armoured Brigades
5th Mechanized Division: 15th, 20th Mechanized, 26th Armoured Brigades
9th Armoured Division: 35th, 43rd Armoured, 14th Mechanized Brigades
33rd Special Forces Brigade
Headquarters 91st, 92nd, 98th Reserve Brigades

30th Border Guard Division: 5th, 6th, 103rd, 104th, 105th, 106th, 107th, 108th, 109th, 110th, 113rd, 115th, 116th Border Guard Brigades

Bibliography

Much of the material presented in this book was obtained in the course of research for earlier books by co-authors covering the topic of air warfare between Iran and Iraq, primarily during interviews with participants and eyewitnesses from Iran and Iraq, but also from Egypt, France and the USA. Sadly, threats against the security of specific persons prevented most of them from speaking openly. Much additional information was compiled with the help of visitors to the ACIG.info forum, who combined their efforts in attempting to research this conflict as closely as possible. The contributions of all those who shared their insights proved precious and enabled us to cross-examine the following publications (as well as those mentioned in footnotes) that were consulted in the preparation of this book:

Books

Alibabaie, G.R., *A History of Iranian Air Force* (in Farsi) (Tehran: Ashian, 2002).
Buchan, James, *Days of God: The revolution in Iran and its consequences* (London: John Murray, 2013).
Cooper, Tom, & Bishop, Farzad, *Iran-Iraq War in the Air 19801988* (Atglen: Schiffer Military History, 2000).
Cordesman, Anthony H., *The Iran-Iraq War and Western Security 19841987* (London: Jane's Publishing Company Ltd, 1987).
Cordesman, Anthony H., & Wagner, Abraham R., *The Lessons of Modern War: Volume II The Iran-Iraq War* (Boulder/San Francisco: Westview Press,

1990/London: Mansell Publishing Ltd, 1990).

Dupuy, Colonel Trevor N., *Elusive Victory: The Arab-Israeli Wars 1947–1974* (London: Macdonald and Jane's Publishers, 1978).

Farouk, Dr Kaveh, *Iran at War 1500–1980* (Botley: Osprey Publishing, 2011).

Foss, Christopher, *Jane's Armour and Artillery, 1980–2007* (Coulsdon: Jane's Information Group, 1980–2007).

Goldsack, Paul (ed.), *Jane's World Railways 1980–1981* (Coulsdon: Jane's Information Group, 1980).

Hiro, Dilip, *The Longest War: The Iran-Iraq Military Conflict* (London: Paladin Grafton Books, 1989).

International Institute for Strategic Studies, *The Military Balance 1980–1982* (London: 1980–1982).

De Lestapis, Jacques (ed.), *Military Powers Encyclopedia, League of Arab States; Irak, Jordan, Lebanon, Syria, PLO, Iran, Israel* (Paris: Society I³C, 1989).

Malovany, Lieutenant Colonel Pesach, *Milhamot Bavel ha-Hadasha (The Wars of Modern Babylon)* (Tel Aviv: Malarakhot, 2010).

Al-Marashi, Ibrahim, & Salama, Sammy, *Iraq's Armed Forces: An analytical history* (London: Routledge, 2009).

Murray, Williamson, & Woods, Kevin M., *The Iran-Iraq War: A Military and Strategic History* (Cambridge: Cambridge University Press, 2014).

National Training Center, *The Iraqi Army: organization and tactics* (Boulder, Colorado: Paladin Press, 1991).

Nejad, Parviz Mosalla (ed.), *Shalamcheh* (Shalamcheh: Sarir Publication, 2006). Downloaded from website Shalamcheh Author: The Hub of Resistance Literature & History (sajed.ir/upload%5Ctopic%5Cebook-Shalamcheh.pdf).

O'Ballance, Edgar, *The Gulf War* (London: Brassey's Defence Publishers, 1988).

Pelletiere, Stephen C., *The Iran-Iraq War: Chaos in a Vacuum* (Westport CT and London: Praeger, 1992).

Pollack, Kenneth M., *Arabs at War. Military effectiveness 1948–1991* (Lincoln and London: University of Nebraska Press, 2002).

Rottman, Gordon L., *The Rocket Propelled Grenade* (Botley: Osprey Publishing, 2010).

Schmidt, Rachel, *Global Arms Exports to Iraq, 1960–1990* (Santa Monica, California: RAND, 1991).

Stockholm International Peace Research Institute (SIPRI), *Yearbooks 1980–1989. World Armaments and Disarmament* (Oxford: Oxford University Press, 1980–1989).

US Arms Control and Disarmament Agency, *World Military Expenditures and Arms Transfers 1972–1982* (Washington DC: 1984).

Ward, Steven R., *Immortal: A military history of Iran and its armed forces* (Washington DC: Georgetown University Press, 2009).

Woods, Kevin M. (with Murray Williamson, Elizabeth A. Nathan, Laila Sabara, Ana M. Veneger), *Saddam's Generals: Perspectives of the Iran-Iraq War* (Alexandria, Va: Institute for Defense Analysis, 2010).

Woods, Kevin M. (with Murray Williamson & Thomas Holaday with Mounir Elkhamri), *Project 1946* (Alexandria, Virginia: Institute for Defense Analyses, 2008).

Woods, Kevin M. (with Murray Williamson & Thomas Holaday with Mounir Elkhamri), *Saddam's War: An Iraqi Military Perspective Of The Iran-Iraq War* (Washington DC: United States Dept. of Defense {McNair Papers}, 2009).

Zabih, Sepehr, *The Iranian military in Revolution and War* (London: Routledge, 1988). New version published 2011 (under author Sepehr Zabir) as part of Routledge Library Editions: Iran, (Abingdon: Routledge, 2011), ISBN 978-0-415-57033-6.

Articles, Essays, Monographs, Papers, Theses

Abramowitz, Jeff, Hahn, Jacqueline, & Cheslow, Jerry, 'Iraq: the military build-up', *IDF Journal*, Vol. III No. 2 (Spring 1986).

Atkeson, Major General Edward B., 'Iraq's Arsenal: Tool of Ambition', *Army* (March 1991), pp.22–30.

Beuttel, H.W., 'Iranian casualties in the Iran-Iraq War: A re-appraisal. Parts 1 & 2', *TNDM*, Vol. 2 No. 3 (December 1997) and Vol. 2 No. 4 (December 1998).

Cooper, Tom, 'La Guerre des Villes: Baghdad contre Téhéran', *Air Combat*, No. 8 (2014).

Cooper, Tom, & Bishop, Farzad, 'Fire in the Hills: Iraq and Iran in Conflict', *Air Enthusiast*, Issue 104 (March/April 2003), pp.14–24.

Cooper, T., & Fontanellaz, A., 'La bataille de Susangerd: Duel de chars dans le Golfe', *Batailles & Blindes Magazine*, No. 57 (2014).

Cooper, T., Sadik, A., & Bishop, F., 'La Guerre Iran-Irak: Les combats aérienns Volume 1', *Avions*, Hors Serie 22 (2007).

Cooper, T., Sadik, A., & Bishop, F., 'La Guerre Iran-Irak: Les combats aérienns Volume 2', *Avions*, Hors Serie 23 (2007).

Davis, Major Mark J., 'Iranians' Operational Warfighting Ability: An Historical Assessment and View to the Future' (Fort Leavenworth, Kansas: School of Advanced Military Studies, United States Army and Command General Staff College, 1992).

Furlong, D.M., 'Iran A power to be reckoned with', *International Defence Review* (June 1973).

Griffin, Lieutenant Colonel Gary B., 'The Iraqi Way of War: An operational assessment' (Fort Leavenworth, Kansas: School of Advanced Military Studies, United States Army Command and General Staff College, 1990).

Lamont, Lieutenant Colonel R.W., 'A Tale of Two Cities – Hue and Khorramshahr', *Armor*, Vol. 108 No. 3 (May–June 1999).

McLaurin, R.D., 'Military Operations in the Gulf War: The Battle of Khorramshahr' (Aberdeen Proving Ground, Maryland: US Army Human Engineering Laboratory, 1982). Cached copy (www.dtic.mil/dtic/tr/fulltext/u2/b067661.pdf.

(No author), 'The international arms industry: Final casualty of the Gulf War', *Jane's Defence Weekly* (30 July 1988).

O'Ballance, Colonel Edgar, 'Iran vs Iraq: Quantity vs Quality?', Defence Attache No. 1 (1987), pp.25–31.

Perkins, Major General K., 'Death of an Army: A short analysis of the Imperial Iranian armed forces', *The RUSI Journal* (June 1980)

Samuel, Annie Tracy, 'Perceptions and Narratives of Security: The Iranian Revolutionary Guards Corps and the Iran-Iraq War', Discussion Paper, June 2012 (Cambridge, Mass: John F. Kennedy School of Government, Harvard University, Belfer Center for Science and International Affairs, 2012).

Tucker, A.R., 'Armored Warfare in the Gulf', *Armed Forces* (May 1988), pp.223–26.

Various periodicals published by the Iranian and Iraqi Ministries of Defence, 1980s, 1990s and 2000s.

Documents

Conflict Record Research Center (CRRC)

SH/GMID/D/000/531: General Military Intelligence Directorate (GMID) Intelligence Reports about Iranian Force Movements during the Iran-Iraq War (April–May 1982).

SH-GMD-D-000-842: MID Report Assessing Political, Military and Economic Conditions in Iran (probably July 1980).

SH-MISC-D-000-827: Saddam and Senior Iraqi Officials Discussing the Conflict with Iran, Iraqi Targets and Plans, a recent Attack on the Osirak Reactor, and Various Foreign Countries (1 October 1980).

SH-MISC-D-001-350: The Passing of Two Years of War: Iran-Iraq, Political Office of the Islamic Revolution Pasdaran Corps.

SH-PDWN-D-001-021: Transcripts of Meetings Between Saddam and Senior Iraqi Officials Discussing Military Tactics During the War with Iran, Including the Use of Napalm and Cluster Bombs, Tank Maneuvering and Attacking Oil Refineries (meeting on 6 October 1980).

SP-PDWN-D-000-552: Documents from the Presidential Diwan regarding arms agreements signed between Iraq and the Soviet Union in 1981 and 1983.

SH–SHTP-A-000-835: Saddam and His Advisors Discussing Iraq's Decision to Go to War with Iran (16 September 1980).

SH-SHTP-D-000-856: Transcript of a Meeting between Saddam Hussein and the Armed Forces General Command (22 November 1980).

Defense Intelligence Agency

DDB-1100-IZ-81: Ground Order of Battle Iraq (March 1981).

DDB-1100-342-86: Ground Forces Intelligence Study Iran (May 1986).

DDB-1100-343-85: Ground Forces Intelligence Study Iraq (November 1985).

DDB-2680-103-88 Part II: Military Intelligence Summary: Volume III, Part II Middle East and North Africa (Persian Gulf) (cut-off date 1 July 1987).

UK National Archives

BT 241/2929: Iran Military Supplies.
FCO 8/2793: Sale of Chieftain tanks from the United Kingdom to Iraq, 1976.
FCO 8/2845: UK Defence Sales to Iraq.
FCO 8/3020: Report of Defence Attaché's, Baghdad, September 1979.
FCO 8/3023: Sale of Chieftain Tanks from UK to Iraq, 1977.
FCO 8/3124: Arms Sales to Iran, 1978.
FCO 8/3135: Sale of Shir Iran Main Battle Tanks to Iran.
FCO 8/3624: Supply of Military Equipment to Iran.
FCO 8/3715: Defence Attaché's Annual Report on Iraq, 1980.
FCO 8/3841: Head of Defence Sales Visits to the Gulf.
FCO 8/4146: Defence sales to Iraq: Tanks.
FCO 8/4156: UK Defence Attache's Annual Report, 1981.
FCO 8/4162: Sale of Barmine and Ranger to Iraq.
FCO 8/4164: Sale of tanks to Iraq.
WO341/204: Report on Shir I (FV 4030).

US Army Intelligence and Security Command

Untitled and undated history of Iran-Iraq War from September 1980 to the spring of 1983.

Released under NGIA FOIA request NGA #20130255F and US Army Intelligence and Security Command request FOIA#2456F-12 on 19 November 2013. Declassified 19 March 2013.

Websites

Ahwaz Climate Climate of Ahwaz, Iran/world climate, www.world-climates.com/city-climate-ahwaz-iran-asia/

AllRefer Country Study and Country Guide, Iran, www.allrefer.com/country-guide-study/iran/iran155.html. Iran The Revolutionary Period and Supreme Defence Council of Iran

Cipher Machines website, www.ciphermachines.com.

Climatological Normals of Abadan, www.hko.gov.hk/wxinfo/climat/world/eng/asia/westasia/abadan_e.htm.

Freemeteo website, www.freemeteo.com. Weather history, Kuwait and Diyarkabir. Daily archive.

www.harvardmun.org/wp-content/uploads/2012/01/JCCIran1.pdf.

www.iiarmy.topcities.com/army/ground/iigf.html (6 February 2003).

Imposed War website, (www.sarjed.ir, or www.english.tebyan.net.

www.ironsides8m.com/army/ir.htm~army.